THE
LOVE & LEMONS
COOKBOOK

THE
LOVE & LEMONS

COOKBOOK

AN APPLE-TO-ZUCCHINI
CELEBRATION OF IMPROMPTU COOKING

JEANINE DONOFRIO

JACK MATHEWS

AVERY

AN IMPRINT OF PENGUIN RANDOM HOUSE
NEW YORK

AVERY

an imprint of Penguin Random House LLC
375 Hudson Street
New York, New York 10014

Most Avery books are available at special quantity discounts for bulk purchase for sales promotions, premiums, fund-raising,
and educational needs. Special books or book excerpts also can be created to fit specific needs. For details, write
SpecialMarkets@penguinrandomhouse.com.

ISBN 978-1-58333-586-4

Printed in China
9   10

BOOK DESIGN BY TRINA BENTLEY OF MAKE & MATTER
FOOD STYLING BY JEANINE DONOFRIO
PROP STYLING BY JENN ELLIOTT BLAKE

To our *Love & Lemons* readers . . .

CONTENTS

WHY LOVE & LEMONS?

Because once, we walked by an Italian dog
with a lemon in its mouth.
Obviously.

Italy. It's part of my ancestry, it's part of my love story, and it's really the beginning of my food story. In 2008, my now-husband Jack and I craved an adventure. We hadn't traveled much together, so, to satisfy our wanderlust, off to Italy we went. Little did I know that Jack had a secret plan. He boarded the plane with a ring in his pocket and he was going to propose. He usually can't keep a secret, but this time he got me. So after dinner, on our first night in Rome, I was suddenly engaged.

But something else happened in Italy—we also fell head over heels for the food. I know . . . it's a pretty cliché story. We were inspired not only by the dishes but by the quality of the ingredients, the care, and the love in everything. Every time I slice into a tomato, I think of the sweetest ones I had on the island of Capri . . . when I stir kale into a hearty soup, I'm immediately taken back to Tuscany. Everything was fresh, vibrant, and bright. Dishes were finished with lemon (and meals were finished with limoncello!). "Simple food, mixed with love for your ingredients" quickly became our new mantra.

This love for food became our true shared passion, and this passion has taken us all over the world. I'll never forget biting into the most tender, sweet, and salty miso eggplant I first had in Kyoto (see my Nasu Dengaku recipe, page 135), snacking on Spanish tortillas and "sometimes spicy" padrón peppers in Barcelona, or sitting on the rooftop of a riad in Marrakech, taking notes about a simple carrot salad.

These experiences made me look at ingredients and their preparation in a new way, which ultimately made me appreciate the local ingredients that are right here in Austin. I found myself visiting local farms and farmers markets, and getting a deep understanding of the vibrant food scene in my own community. As I started to cook locally and seasonally, I felt a sense of place with my food, and it became something I wanted to share.

We started the *Love & Lemons* blog as a place to share not only my recipes but the idea of local seasonal cooking. I generally make food inspired by the place that I live (hence the fact that there are no fewer than five taco recipes in this book), and I hope to inspire others to do the same.

So what about the dog, then? As we were coming up with names for the food blog, we both remembered an idyllic afternoon walk in Capri, where this love story truly began, when a golden retriever trotted past us with a lemon in its mouth. We joked about the romantic notion that Italians probably play fetch with lemons instead of tennis balls.

IMPATIENT—I MEAN—IMPROMPTU COOKING

While our travels sparked my passion to get into the kitchen, something always stopped me from being a practical, everyday sort of cook. I'd get frustrated trying to plan and shop for a week's worth of meals—a certain vegetable wouldn't be available at the store, I'd forget an ingredient that was on my list, or I'd simply not feel like eating what I planned to make on Thursday by the time Thursday rolled around. I enjoyed spending time cooking on Sundays, but I couldn't get it together to easily eat at home Monday through Friday. Until one day I did.

Eventually, I figured out that Sunday's leftover vegetables could be quickly tossed into Monday's scrambled eggs or Tuesday's pasta. I didn't suddenly become a list maker . . . instead something clicked in my mind where I could turn one night's dinner into another day's breakfast into another day's lunch, and so on. I figured out how to use ingredients in resourceful ways that still left a little room for last-minute cravings and creativity. I'd finally found food-making freedom. Maybe you're a pro (chef or mom or otherwise) and you know these things already, but as I learned them, they felt like rocket science to me.

So here goes . . .

COOK BACKWARD.

We've all been there—you head to the store with an asparagus recipe and there's no asparagus to be found . . . You get home and realize you forgot to get basil . . . Your CSA box arrives with a cauliflower bigger than your head . . . Those carrots at the farmers market are so pretty, but how the heck do you turn carrots into an actual dinner?

That's why this book is not organized by breakfast, lunch, and dinner—it's organized by vegetable so that you can come home with something beautiful from the farmers market and then figure out what to make with it. Or you can start with a vegetable or two that you have on hand and build from there.

Every vegetable under the sun isn't represented here. These recipes include some of my favorite ingredients as well as the fruits and vegetables that happen to be available in my area in central Texas.

USE LOCAL, SEASONAL PRODUCE WHENEVER YOU CAN.

Some things are especially worth waiting for—a just-picked summer tomato, a super-sweet spring strawberry, or a drip-down-your-arm Texas peach. I love how the local carrots are sweeter, the young leeks are melt-in-your-mouth tender, and the peppers here are you-better-not-touch-your-eye spicy. Kale will always be one of my favorite vegetables, but have you tried amaranth, dandelion, or sweet potato greens? I love exploring my markets from season to season and I hope to inspire you to get acquainted with your local produce. There's nothing like bicolored corn in the Midwest in August, chanterelle mushrooms in Seattle in September, and ramps and rhubarb in the Northeast in the spring.

SEASONAL FOOD STILL NEEDS SEASONING.

I used to have this misconception that restaurant food would always taste better than anything I could cook at home. And then I realized that I was just under-seasoning my food. Generous (yet appropriate) amounts of sea salt and pepper, coupled with some squeezes of lemon, make simple foods instantly more delicious.

The recipes in this book call for sea salt, which I prefer because its flavor is less bitter than standard iodized table salt. As for pepper, I recommend using whole black peppercorns freshly ground from your pepper mill.

If you're cooking from this book, I can only assume that you love bright, vibrant food as much as I do. Lemons, limes, and vinegars will really bring your food to life. Always, always use lemon juice fresh from an actual lemon; never buy it in a bottle.

TAKE RECIPES WITH A GRAIN OF SALT (PUN INTENDED).

My intention with this book is for it to give you ideas. I'm a very visual person and sometimes all I need to get out of a cooking rut is to see a picture of a beautiful vegetable dish. So I hope you can take these pictures and simple recipes and use them as inspiration to get creative in your own kitchen. Feel free to put your own unique spin on things using good ingredients that you have available, adapting to your own taste preferences as you go.

LOVE VEGETABLES.

I love vegetables. Everything about them. Of course they're healthy and they make you feel good when you eat them, but there's so much more. I love the way roasting butternut squash makes my kitchen smell like Thanksgiving . . . the way the colors of zucchini, yellow squash, and bright red bell peppers become a rainbow of ratatouille in a skillet . . . the way onions sound when they sizzle the second they touch the pan.

This is a book about vegetables. The recipes are entirely vegetarian, but that doesn't mean you have to be. Whether you're vegan, vegetarian, pesceterian, or a meat-on-the-side-ian, since you're reading this book I assume that you appreciate a new vegetable recipe as much as I do. I hope that you find some delicious plant-based inspiration within these pages. So let's get cooking, shall we?

LO

&

JEANINE DONOFRIO

LEM

AVERY AN IMPRI

2 0

IMPROM

APPLES

OOKING

VE
ONS

JACK MATHEWS

F PENGUIN RANDOM HOUSE   NEW YORK

16

UCCHINI

HOW TO COOK WITH WHAT YOU HAVE

My basic guide for impromptu cooking

1

START WITH THE VEGETABLES

Instead of going to the store with a recipe in hand, try making dinner with what you have *on hand*. I visit my farmers market weekly and also get a bi-weekly CSA box. Having fresh fruits, vegetables, and herbs readily available in your kitchen is the first step to building easy, healthy meals.

2

CHOOSE A MEAL FORMAT

Once you have a vegetable (or two or three) picked out, look to your pantry to decide what form the meal will take. For example, if I have tortillas on hand, it's taco night; if I have vegetable stock, soup's on!

3

SUPPORTING INGREDIENTS

Take a second look around your kitchen and see what supporting ingredients you can add for balance and flavor. Chickpeas are an easy pantry-based protein, a slice of avocado is a delicious healthy fat, roasted red bell peppers add flavor to a frittata, and pickled onions add pop to a quesadilla.

When I'm trying to put dinner on the table without an extra trip to the store, this is my general approach. This process might feel backward if you're used to heading to the store with a recipe in hand. If you're not used to cooking backward, it'll take some practice. Once you get the hang of it, though, it's fun and freeing, not to mention efficient and time-saving!

4

SAUCE IT UP

So many meals are made better with a sauce or a dressing, be it salsa for Mexican food, peanut sauce for soba noodles, or a dollop of pesto on toast. Of course, sometimes all you really need is a drizzle of olive oil and a squeeze of lemon.

TIP:

Whenever you take time to make a sauce, make extra and you'll be ahead of the game tomorrow!

5

SPICE, GIRL

Don't be afraid to kick up the flavors in your food with spice. Hot or not, experiment by adding curry or chili powders to your quinoa salads, chipotle peppers to your pesto, or a squirt of sriracha on your omelette. In a pinch, a few pinches of red pepper flakes will always do.

6

PAY IT FORWARD

Use what you make as a jumping-off point for the next day's meal. Extra roasted vegetables can go into tomorrow's enchiladas. Extra hummus can elevate tomorrow's sandwich or wrap. It's time to get creative!

WHAT TO MAKE WHEN YOU HAVE MANY VEGETABLES

EVERYTHING EGGS

Half of a zucchini, a handful of cherry tomatoes, a small piece of red onion, or a few scallions. What these leftover ingredients have in common is that they're all perfect when folded into creamy scrambled eggs. Top your eggs with leftover herbs and freshly cracked black pepper. Stuff this all into a tortilla and you have a quick breakfast taco.

JUST ADD TORTILLAS

In my book, anything can be wrapped up in a tortilla to become a complete meal. Leftover grilled zucchini, roasted mushrooms, red bell peppers, or sweet potatoes are all taco-worthy. Add a slice of avocado, a squeeze of lime, and a scoop of salsa.

KITCHEN SINK SALAD

Salad doesn't have to be rabbit food. Toss greens with a hearty grain like quinoa or farro. Add raw or roasted vegetables, cheeses, nuts, and fresh or dried fruits. Drizzle it all with olive oil, apple cider vinegar, or a big squeeze of lemon and season generously with salt and pepper.

While the recipes in this book are generally created with a "hero" vegetable in mind, there are undoubtedly times when you will have many things to use up. Here are six of my most flexible go-to veggie-ful meals that you can't go (too) wrong with any day of the week. No measuring allowed.

VEGGIE-FUL PASTA

Any vegetables you have—roasted, grilled, or raw—can become a complete meal when tossed with pasta and some extras. In the fall, I lean toward heartier ingredients like butternut squash, kale, feta cheese, and sage. In the summer, I keep it fresh with peels of zucchini, sliced tomatoes, and fresh mozzarella. Top with pesto or simply toss with fresh herbs, lemon juice, and olive oil. Dinner is re-served.

MANY-VEGETABLE SOUP

At the end of the week when my produce isn't exactly the freshest, I like to make soup. Start by sautéing onion and garlic in extra-virgin olive oil with a few pinches of sea salt. Next, add the vegetables that need the most time to cook—carrots, cubed butternut squash, or chopped kale stems—and cook until tender. Season with salt and pepper and add dry herbs and spices of your choice (thyme, oregano, cumin, etc.). Add a splash of white wine, freshly diced or canned tomatoes, and vegetable broth. Simmer for 20 minutes, then add leafy vegetables (spinach, kale, chard) and stir until wilted.

WHAT TO HAVE ON HAND AT ALL TIMES

Or at least most of the time

ESSENTIALS

Oils
coconut oil
extra-virgin olive oil
toasted sesame oil

Vinegars
apple cider vinegar
balsamic vinegar
rice vinegar
sherry vinegar
white wine vinegar

Seasoning
sea salt
whole black peppercorns

Sweeteners
maple syrup and/or honey
raw cane sugar

FROM THE BULK BINS

Dry Herbs & Spices
cayenne pepper
chili powder
cinnamon
curry powder
dried oregano
ground coriander
ground cumin
red pepper flakes
smoked paprika
whole nutmeg

Grains
brown, jasmine, or basmati rice
farro or wheat berries
quinoa, any color
rolled oats
white all-purpose flour
whole spelt flour
whole wheat flour

Nuts & Seeds
almonds
blanched hazelnuts
hemp seeds
peanuts
pepitas
pine nuts
pistachios
raw cashews
raw sunflower seeds
walnuts

GROCERY STAPLES

Fridge
almond milk
Dijon mustard
eggs, preferably organic
feta cheese
fresh mozzarella cheese
Parmesan or pecorino cheese

Pantry
beans, dried or canned
canned chipotles in adobo sauce
canned diced tomatoes
coconut milk
green or red curry paste
jarred roasted red bell peppers
soba noodles
sriracha or sambal
tahini
tamari
variety of pastas and couscous
vermicelli rice noodles
white miso paste

Fresh Staples
corn or flour tortillas
fresh whole-grain bread
garlic
ginger
lemons and limes
onions or shallots
rotation of fresh herbs

COOKING TOOLS

The Basics

1 good chef's knife that fits comfortably in your hand

paring knife

serrated knife

wood cutting board

stainless steel pots and pans

large Dutch oven

10- or 12-inch cast-iron skillet

cast-iron grill pan

nonstick ceramic skillet

baking sheets and pans

Handheld

wooden spoons

metal tongs

silicone spatulas

whisks—small and large

vegetable peeler

julienne peeler

Microplane zester

box or handheld grater

Japanese mandoline

Prep

measuring spoons and cups

glass bowls in many sizes

small prep bowls

colander and a fine mesh strainer

Power

high-speed blender

small food processor

stand mixer

Extras

waffle maker

ice-cream maker

rice cooker

While the items listed here are used throughout the recipes in this book, don't feel the need to have absolutely everything stocked in your kitchen at all times. I sure don't. Many ingredients are interchangeable. For example, there's no need to run to the store to get farro for a farro salad if you have wheat berries. Pesto is traditionally made with pine nuts, but walnuts, pistachios, and even pepitas substitute well and will change up your routine. After all, variety is the spice of life.

1

APPLES

⸺●━━━━━━━━━━●⸺

When fall approaches, I think back to my family's annual apple-picking trips to the local orchard. We'd gather bushel after bushel, eating more apples than any doctor would probably recommend. Afterward, we'd order pizzas and settle in for a long evening of apple pie making. To be honest, I think I did more of the eating than the making because my sister is the one who is skilled in the art of patience and pastry. These days, while I have a foolproof apple crisp recipe, I especially love to use apples in unexpected savory ways—chipotle apple guacamole (page 9), apple radish slaw (page 11), and veggie ceviche (page 113).

SEASON

⸺⸺⸺⸺

FALL

Try using
other fruits,
such as pear,
fig, and dried
cranberry.

APPLE, BRIE & THYME CROSTINI

INGREDIENTS

8 slices ciabatta bread

8 (¼-inch/0.5-cm) slices brie cheese

1 Gala apple, thinly sliced

Extra-virgin olive oil, for drizzling

Honey, for drizzling

4 sprigs fresh thyme, thick woody stems removed

Sea salt and freshly ground black pepper

DIRECTIONS

Preheat the oven to 350°F (180°C) and line a large baking sheet with parchment paper. Place the ciabatta slices on the baking sheet and top each with a slice of brie, a few slices of apple, and a drizzle of olive oil. Bake until the cheese is melted and the bread is toasted. Remove from the oven and drizzle each crostini with honey. Top with a sprig of fresh thyme, season with salt and pepper, and serve hot.

SERVES: 4

Toast became a crazy trend, and I think for good reason—who doesn't like things topped on bread? It's simple, delicious, and easy to elevate with just a few ingredients. My crostini combination formula looks like this:
1 part savory + 1 part sweet + 1 part fresh herb.

TIP:

This is also delicious with pears, peaches, or mixed berries. Bake time will vary depending on the fruit.

CARDAMOM APPLE CRISP

3 small Gala apples, cored and chopped

Juice of ½ small lemon

⅓ cup (75 mL) whole rolled oats

⅓ cup (75 mL) chopped walnuts

¼ cup (60 mL) spelt or whole wheat flour

⅓ cup (75 mL) brown sugar

½ teaspoon (2 mL) cinnamon

¼ teaspoon (1 mL) ground cardamom

¼ teaspoon (1 mL) salt

3 tablespoons (45 mL) butter or hardened coconut oil

¼ cup (60 mL) dried tart cherries or cranberries (optional)

Preheat the oven to 375°F (190°C). Brush the bottoms of four small ramekins with coconut oil.

In a medium bowl, toss the chopped apples with the lemon juice.

In a small bowl, mix together the oats, walnuts, flour, brown sugar, cinnamon, cardamom, and salt.

Cut the butter or hardened coconut oil into a few small pieces. Using your hands, work the butter into the flour mixture until well combined but still crumbly.

Mix the apples and dried tart cherries, if using, with half of the crumble mixture and divide evenly into 4 small ramekins. Sprinkle the rest of the crumble on top of each one.

Bake for 35 minutes, or until the apples are soft and the crumble is golden brown.

Let sit for 15 to 20 minutes before serving. Serve with scoops of ice cream.

VEGAN: Use coconut oil.

GLUTEN-FREE: Use oat flour in place of spelt or whole wheat.

SERVES: **4**

APPLE FENNEL SALAD

DRESSING

2 tablespoons (30 mL) extra-virgin olive oil

1½ tablespoons (22 mL) fresh lemon juice

2 tablespoons (30 mL) fresh orange juice

½ teaspoon (2 mL) Dijon mustard

Sea salt and freshly ground black pepper

- -

2 fennel bulbs, thinly sliced

1 Gala apple, thinly sliced

4 radishes, thinly sliced

⅓ cup (75 mL) chopped scallions

3 cups (750 mL) baby salad greens

¼ cup (60 mL) fresh mint leaves

⅓ cup (75 mL) crumbled feta cheese

⅓ cup (75 mL) sliced almonds

Make the dressing: In a small bowl, whisk together the olive oil, lemon juice, orange juice, and Dijon mustard. Season with salt and pepper.

Assemble the salad: In a large bowl, toss the fennel, apple, radishes, scallions, and baby salad greens with half of the dressing until well coated. Add the mint, cheese, and almonds and toss to combine. Taste and season with salt and pepper, and the additional dressing, if desired.

| NOTE | Use a mandoline, if you have one, to slice the fennel, apple, and radishes paper-thin. |

VEGAN: Skip the cheese. | **GLUTEN-FREE** | *SERVES:* **4**

CHIPOTLE APPLE GUACAMOLE

INGREDIENTS	DIRECTIONS
3 ripe avocados Juice of 1 to 2 limes 1 Fuji or Gala apple, diced 1 chipotle pepper, chopped, from canned chipotles in adobo sauce 1 tablespoon (15 mL) adobo sauce ½ cup (125 mL) chopped cilantro Sea salt	Peel and pit the avocados and scoop them into a medium bowl. Add the lime juice and a few generous pinches of salt. Use the back of a large fork to mash the avocado until the ingredients are incorporated but not completely smooth. Fold in the apple, chipotle, adobo sauce, and cilantro. Season to taste with more salt and lime juice as desired. Serve with tortilla chips and margaritas!

VEGAN | **GLUTEN-FREE**

SERVES: **4**

I like to make guacamole that changes with the seasons—mango in the spring, watermelon in the summer, and I especially love this version with apples in the fall. Chipotle peppers add a spicy, smoky kick.

1 Slice the apple into 4 sections around the core.

2 Slice the sections into very thin planks.

3 Slice the planks into 1-inch matchsticks.

4 Repeat with radishes and toss the slaw together.

APPLE RADISH SLAW

1 Gala apple

8 to 10 small red radishes

4 scallions, chopped small (½ cup/125 mL)

Juice of 1 lime

½ teaspoon (2 mL) extra-virgin olive oil

½ cup (125 mL) chopped cilantro

Sea salt and freshly ground black pepper

Slice the apple into 4 sections around the core. Slice the first section into very thin planks, then stack the planks and slice them horizontally into thin 1-inch matchsticks. Repeat for each section, slicing the rest of the apple. Slice the radishes into very thin planks, then stack the planks and slice them horizontally into matchsticks, matching the size of the apple matchsticks.

In a medium bowl, combine the sliced apple, radishes, scallions, lime juice, olive oil, cilantro, a pinch of salt, and freshly ground pepper. Toss to coat. Chill for 30 minutes. After chilling, season the slaw with additional salt and pepper to taste.

TIP   Serve with portobello sliders (page 169), or on the side of whatever you're grilling!

VEGAN | **GLUTEN-FREE**

SERVES: **4** *AS A SIDE*

ARTICHOKES

2

Fresh artichokes take some work to prepare, but they're oh so worth it. My number one tip for fresh artichokes: Keep them simple so you can really taste the fruits (er, vegetables) of your labor. If you're making artichoke dip or hummus (page 227), go ahead and use canned or jarred artichokes. Save your fresh ones to eat simply with lemon and olive oil, or top them on a crostini.

SEASON

SPRING

| **1** | Slice the top and peel off dark green leaves. |

| **2** | Use a paring knife to slice off the woody part of the stem. |

| **3** | Slice the artichoke in half and use a spoon to remove the fuzzy choke. |

| **4** | Place in a bowl of lemon water until ready to use. |

HOW TO CLEAN
AND PREP ARTICHOKES

1 lemon

8 fresh baby artichokes

Fill a large bowl with water and add the juice of one lemon. Quarter the lemon and add it to the water. Transfer the artichokes to the lemon water as you work.

Cut off the top quarter of the artichokes, about 1 inch (2.5 cm). Remove and discard the first 3 to 4 layers of dark green outer leaves. Trim the stems to ½ inch (1 cm), then use a paring knife to peel away the woody part of the stems. Slice the artichokes in half lengthwise. Use a small spoon to remove the fuzzy chokes from each half.

Leave the artichokes in the lemon water until you're ready to use them.

TIP : *Always keep sliced artichokes in lemon water to prevent them from browning.*

LEMON-ROASTED ARTICHOKES

8 baby artichokes

1 lemon

3 tablespoons (45 mL) extra-virgin olive oil

Sea salt and freshly ground black pepper

Preheat the oven to 375°F (190°C).

Clean and prep the artichokes according to the instructions on page 15.

Brush a large baking pan with 1 tablespoon (15 mL) of olive oil. Gently drain the artichokes and lemons, then place them back in the bowl. Add the remaining olive oil and generous pinches of salt and pepper. Gently toss with your hands to coat evenly. Place the artichokes cut side down in the baking pan, add the quartered lemon, and cover with foil. Bake 25 to 30 minutes, or until the leaves are tender and the cut sides are nicely browned.

Serve with the roasted lemons.

VEGAN | **GLUTEN-FREE**

SERVES: 4

ARTICHOKE CROSTINI
WITH MINT PESTO

1 recipe lemon-roasted artichokes
(page 17)

1 cup (250 mL) mint pesto (page 275)

8 slices whole-grain bread

Extra-virgin olive oil, for drizzling

½ garlic clove

16 mint leaves

Pinches of red pepper flakes

Sea salt and freshly ground black pepper

Roast the artichokes and make the
mint pesto.

Preheat the oven to 400°F (200°C). Place
the bread on a large baking sheet and
drizzle with olive oil. Bake for 10 to
12 minutes, or until toasted and golden.

Remove from the oven and rub each piece
with the cut side of the garlic clove. Place
the bread on a serving platter and top
each piece with a slather of mint pesto,
1 artichoke heart sliced in half, 2 mint
leaves, red pepper flakes, and salt and
pepper to taste.

VEGAN | **GLUTEN-FREE**

SERVES: **4**

This is my favorite crostini to make in the springtime, when baby
artichokes show up at the farmers market. The bright, lemony
mint pesto perfectly highlights the fresh artichokes.

3

Asparagus

MY FAVORITE WAYS
TO USE ASPARAGUS:

—Grill them as a side dish.
—Blanch and toss them into cold salads.
—Peel them into ribbons and twirl with noodles.
—Chop and fold them into eggs.

SEASON

SPRING

TIP:

If you have extra white bean puree, save it to spread on a sandwich the next day.

FLATBREAD WITH WHITE BEAN PUREE & ASPARAGUS RIBBONS

WHITE BEAN PUREE

1½ cups (375 mL) cooked cannellini beans, drained and rinsed (page 285)

2 tablespoons (30 mL) extra-virgin olive oil

3 tablespoons (45 mL) fresh lemon juice

1 small garlic clove

Sea salt and freshly ground black pepper

- -

4 pieces pita bread or naan

Extra-virgin olive oil, for drizzling

1 bunch of asparagus, tough ends removed

½ teaspoon (2 mL) fresh lemon juice

¼ cup (60 mL) crumbled feta cheese

Small bunch of fresh mint

¼ cup (60 mL) pine nuts, toasted (page 285)

¼ teaspoon (1 mL) lemon zest

Pinch of red pepper flakes

Sea salt and freshly ground black pepper

Make the white bean puree: In a food processor, combine the cannellini beans, olive oil, lemon juice, garlic, and a few generous pinches of salt and pepper. Season to taste. Chill until ready to use.

Preheat the oven to 400°F (200°C). Place the bread on a large rimmed baking sheet and drizzle with olive oil. Bake for 10 minutes, or until toasted and golden brown.

Use a peeler to shave the asparagus into ribbons. Toss them in a bowl with a drizzle of olive oil, the lemon juice, and pinches of salt and pepper.

Spread the white bean puree onto the flatbreads and top each with a few asparagus ribbons, the cheese, mint, pine nuts, lemon zest, and red pepper flakes. Season to taste with salt and pepper.

VEGAN: Skip the cheese.

SERVES: **4**

MILLET PILAF WITH HERBS & GRILLED ASPARAGUS

4 large eggs

1 bunch of asparagus, tough ends removed

1 lemon, sliced in half

Extra-virgin olive oil, for drizzling

2 cups (500 mL) cooked millet (page 284)

⅓ cup (75 mL) walnuts, toasted and chopped (page 285)

1 tablespoon (15 mL) capers

¼ cup (60 mL) chopped chives

1 cup (250 mL) chopped fresh herbs (basil, oregano, and/or thyme)

Sea salt and freshly ground black pepper

Make soft-boiled eggs: Fill a medium pot with water and heat to a gentle simmer, just below boiling. Using a slotted spoon, carefully lower the eggs into the water and let simmer for 8 minutes. Remove and chill immediately in a bowl of ice water for about 3 minutes. Once the eggs are cooled, tap the bottom of each egg to crack a little bit of the shell. Take a small spoon and carefully slide it in and around the egg to loosen and remove it from the shell. Set the peeled eggs aside.

Heat a grill pan over medium-high heat. Drizzle the asparagus and lemon halves with olive oil and season with salt and pepper. Place both on the grill (lemons cut side down). Rotate the asparagus occasionally, until evenly charred, about 8 minutes. Remove from the grill and set aside.

Toss the millet with the walnuts, capers, chives, and herbs. Squeeze the grilled lemon over the pilaf and season with salt and pepper to taste. Divide into 4 portions and top each with the grilled asparagus and one soft-boiled egg.

VEGAN: Skip the eggs. | **GLUTEN-FREE** | *SERVES:* **4**

TIP: This is a picnic-perfect salad. The crunchy ingredients keep well, and you can make it a day or two ahead of time.

ASPARAGUS EDAMAME
SALAD WITH TARRAGON

1 bunch of asparagus, tough ends removed, chopped into 1-inch (2.5-cm) pieces (about 2 cups/500 mL)

2 cups (500 mL) frozen edamame, thawed

¼ cup (60 mL) chopped tarragon

¼ cup (60 mL) chopped mint

4 radishes, thinly sliced

¼ cup (60 mL) pine nuts

Shavings of pecorino cheese (optional)

- -

DRESSING

1½ tablespoons (22 mL) extra-virgin olive oil

1½ tablespoons (22 mL) fresh lemon juice, plus more as needed

1 garlic clove, minced

Sea salt and freshly ground black pepper

Prepare a large pot of boiling water and a large bowl of ice water. Drop the asparagus into the boiling water and blanch for about 45 seconds. With a slotted spoon, remove the asparagus and immediately immerse in the ice water to stop the cooking process. Keep in the ice water long enough to cool completely, about 15 seconds. Drain and place on paper towels to dry.

Make the dressing: In a small bowl, whisk together the olive oil, lemon juice, garlic, and pinches of salt and pepper.

Assemble the salad: In a large bowl, combine the asparagus, edamame, tarragon, mint, and radishes. Toss the salad with the dressing, pine nuts, and pecorino cheese, if using. Season with salt, pepper, and more lemon juice to taste.

VEGAN | **GLUTEN-FREE**

SERVES: **4**

TIP:

Keep avocado halves from browning by storing your cut avocado with a slice of onion in a plastic bag in the fridge.

AVOC

4

ADOS

Quick snack:

Smash sliced avocado on toast with
salt, pepper, a squeeze of lemon, and
some microgreens. Sprinkle hemp
seeds on top for a little protein.

SEASON

VARIES

1 | Crack and whisk the eggs.

2 | Pour the eggs into the skillet, then add the scallions and the spinach.

3 | Gently fold the eggs over the spinach mixture, scrambling the eggs.

4 | Assemble tacos with eggs, avocado, and salsa.

AVOCADO BREAKFAST TACOS

INGREDIENTS	DIRECTIONS
4 large eggs	In a medium bowl, whisk the eggs. In a large nonstick skillet, heat the oil over medium heat. Pour the eggs into the pan. Quickly add a few pinches of salt and pepper, then add the scallions and spinach. Use a silicone spatula to scrape the edges of the pan and gently fold the eggs over the scallions and spinach. Continue to fold until the eggs are scrambled and the spinach is wilted.
½ teaspoon (2 mL) extra-virgin olive oil	
2 scallions, sliced	
2 cups (500 mL) packed baby spinach	
4 tortillas, corn or flour	
1 small avocado, cut into 4 slices	
Creamy tomatillo salsa (page 281)	Divide the scrambled eggs among 4 tortillas. On top of each taco, place one slice of avocado and a spoonful of tomatillo salsa.
Sea salt and freshly ground black pepper	

GLUTEN-FREE: Use corn tortillas.

SERVES: **4**

Simply put, if you live in Austin, you eat breakfast tacos. And often. They're not always healthy, which is why I like to make my own veggie versions at home. This one with spinach, avocado, and spicy tomatillo salsa is a well-balanced meal.

Few things in life are better than the trifecta of tomatoes, fresh mozzarella, and basil. But life just got a little sweeter, because adding avocado and strawberries takes your caprese salad to another level.

AVOCADO STRAWBERRY CAPRESE

¼ cup (60 mL) balsamic vinegar

1 cup (250 mL) sliced strawberries

1 cup (250 mL) halved cherry tomatoes

1 cup (250 mL) halved mini mozzarella balls

1 ripe avocado, pitted and diced

⅓ cup (75 mL) pecans, toasted (page 285)

⅓ cup (75 mL) loosely packed basil, torn

Extra-virgin olive oil, for drizzling

Sea salt and freshly ground black pepper

In a small saucepan, bring the balsamic vinegar to a high simmer over medium heat. Stir, then reduce the heat to low and simmer until the vinegar has thickened and reduced by half, 8 to 10 minutes. Set aside to cool.

Place the strawberries, cherry tomatoes, mozzarella, avocado, pecans, and basil in a shallow bowl or on a platter. Drizzle with olive oil and season generously with salt and pepper. Gently toss. Drizzle with the reduced balsamic.

VEGAN: Skip the cheese. | **GLUTEN-FREE**

SERVES: **4**

AVOCADO & FAVA BEAN SALAD

INGREDIENTS

½ cup (125 mL) fresh fava beans, shelled and peeled

1 medium fennel bulb, thinly sliced

1½ cups (375 mL) sunflower sprouts

½ cup (125 mL) cooked chickpeas, drained and rinsed (page 285)

Extra-virgin olive oil, for drizzling

Juice of ½ small lemon

½ avocado, diced

¼ cup (60 mL) chopped almonds, toasted (page 285)

¼ cup (60 mL) large shavings of Parmesan cheese

Sea salt and freshly ground black pepper

DIRECTIONS

Prepare a small pot of salted boiling water and a small bowl of ice water. Drop the fava beans into the boiling water and blanch for 3 minutes. Remove the beans and immediately immerse them in the ice water to stop the cooking process. Keep the beans in the ice water long enough to cool completely, about 15 seconds. Drain and place on paper towels to dry.

Thinly slice the fennel (using a mandoline, if you have one). Place the fennel slices in a large bowl with the sunflower sprouts, chickpeas, and fava beans. Drizzle the salad with olive oil and the lemon juice and season with salt and pepper. Toss the salad, then add the avocado, almonds, and Parmesan cheese shavings and gently toss again. Taste and adjust the seasonings.

NOTE If you can't find good, fresh sunflower sprouts, substitute them with any kind of soft baby salad green.

VEGAN: Skip the cheese. | **GLUTEN-FREE** | *SERVES:* 4

DARK CHOCOLATE AVOCADO MOUSSE

2 very ripe avocados

4 ounces (125 g) 70% cacao baking chocolate, melted

¼ cup (60 mL) unsweetened cocoa powder

6 tablespoons (90 mL) maple syrup

⅓ cup (75 mL) almond milk

½ teaspoon (2 mL) vanilla extract

¼ teaspoon (1 mL) cinnamon

Sea salt

Coconut cream (page 287)

1 cup (250 mL) raspberries

DIRECTIONS

In a food processor, combine the avocados, melted chocolate, cocoa powder, maple syrup, almond milk, vanilla, cinnamon, and a pinch of salt. Puree until creamy. Spoon the mousse into 4 small ramekins and chill for at least 1 hour.

Serve the mousse topped with a dollop of coconut cream and the raspberries.

VEGAN | **GLUTEN-FREE**

SERVES: **4**

My husband, Jack, isn't the biggest fan of avocados. I prep this one while he's not looking, and he's yet to realize that this decadent chocolaty dessert is made from pureed avocado.

Quick snack: fresh berries over yogurt and granola.

MY FAVORITE SIMPLE GRANOLA RECIPE

Preheat the oven to 300°F (150°C). In a medium bowl, mix together 2 cups (500 mL) rolled oats, ½ cup (125 mL) chopped almonds, 2 teaspoons (10 mL) cinnamon, and ½ teaspoon (2 mL) sea salt. Stir in 2 tablespoons (30 mL) melted coconut oil, ¼ cup (60 mL) maple syrup, and 2 tablespoons (30 mL) almond butter. Spread onto a baking sheet and bake for 30 minutes or until golden brown, tossing halfway through. Let cool. Serve with yogurt and berries!

5

Berries

When berries are perfectly in season,
I say don't do much with them. Keep it simple
and let their sweetness shine. Cut up fresh
strawberries and toss them into a salad or top a
crostini with beautiful fresh blackberries. When
they're out of season, keep raspberries and
blueberries in the freezer for smoothies
(page 282) and ice creams.

SEASON

——————

SPRING / SUMMER

STRAWBERRY SALAD WITH TOASTED HAZELNUTS

SWEET LEMON VINAIGRETTE

2 tablespoons (30 mL) extra-virgin olive oil

2 teaspoons (10 mL) fresh lemon juice

2 teaspoons (10 mL) white balsamic vinegar

2 teaspoons (10 mL) honey or maple syrup

Sea salt and freshly ground black pepper

- -

1½ cups (375 mL) cooked hard or soft wheat berries (page 284)

4 cups (1 L) loosely packed mache greens or baby salad greens

⅓ cup (75 mL) hazelnuts, toasted and chopped (page 285)

1½ cups (375 mL) sliced strawberries

¼ cup (60 mL) sliced radishes

¼ cup (60 mL) sliced basil

¼ cup (60 mL) whole mint leaves

⅓ cup (75 mL) crumbled feta cheese

Make the vinaigrette: In a small bowl, whisk together the olive oil, lemon juice, white balsamic vinegar, and honey. Season with salt and pepper.

Assemble the salad: In a large bowl, combine the wheat berries, mache greens, hazelnuts, strawberries, radishes, basil, mint, and feta cheese. Drizzle the vinaigrette over the salad and toss. Taste and adjust the seasonings.

VEGAN: Skip the cheese and the honey.

GLUTEN-FREE: Use quinoa or millet instead of wheat berries.

SERVES: **4**

I also love
this with fresh
strawberries or
sliced peaches.

BLACKBERRY BASIL BRUSCHETTA

INGREDIENTS

1 cup (250 mL) fresh blackberries

½ teaspoon (2 mL) balsamic vinegar

6 to 8 slices of crusty bread

Extra-virgin olive oil, for drizzling

½ garlic clove

1 (8-ounce/225-g) ball fresh mozzarella, sliced

Handful of fresh basil, thinly sliced

Honey, for drizzling

Sea salt and freshly ground black pepper

DIRECTIONS

Place the blackberries in a small bowl and drizzle with the balsamic vinegar, a pinch of salt, and freshly ground black pepper. Use your hands to gently break them apart. Set aside to macerate for about 10 minutes, or until the blackberries are soft and juicy.

Meanwhile, toast or grill the bread. While it's still warm, drizzle the bread with olive oil and rub with the cut side of the garlic clove.

Top the toasted bread with slices of mozzarella, the blackberries, basil, drizzles of honey, and a pinch of salt and pepper.

SERVES: **4**

PB&J WITH HAZELNUT BUTTER & STRAWBERRY CHIA JAM

HAZELNUT-PECAN BUTTER

1½ cups (375 mL) roasted hazelnuts
(page 285), cooled to room temperature

1½ cups (375 mL) raw pecans

1 to 2 tablespoons (15 to 30 mL) maple syrup

Sea salt

Yield: 1½ cups (375 mL)

STRAWBERRY CHIA JAM

1 pound (500 g) strawberries (about 3 cups)

½ teaspoon (2 mL) fresh lemon juice

2 tablespoons (30 mL) maple syrup

2 to 3 tablespoons (30 to 45 mL) chia seeds

Sea salt

Yield: 1½ cups (375 mL)

8 slices bread, for assembling sandwiches

Make the hazelnut-pecan butter: In a high-speed blender (or good-quality food processor), blend the hazelnuts and pecans until creamy. Stop and scrape down the mixture often, giving your blender a break every few minutes when the motor gets hot. Your nut butter should become creamy after 10 to 15 minutes of blend time. Add the maple syrup and a pinch of salt and blend well.

Make the strawberry chia jam: Remove the stems and slice the strawberries. In a medium saucepan over medium heat, simmer the strawberries and lemon juice for 3 to 5 minutes, stirring often. Break them up gently with a masher or a fork. Add the maple syrup and a pinch of salt and remove from the heat. Stir in the chia seeds and transfer to a glass jar. Let cool slightly, then set in the fridge to chill. If your jam isn't set enough, stir in more chia seeds.

Make sandwiches and store the extra nut butter and jam in glass jars in the refrigerator for up to 1 week.

VEGAN

SERVES: **4**

BLUEBERRY MANGO & MINT ICE CREAM

2 (14-ounce/414-mL) cans full-fat coconut milk, refrigerated overnight

1 heaping cup (265 to 280 mL) blueberries

1 mango, pitted and diced

5 to 7 fresh mint leaves

1½ tablespoons (22 mL) cornstarch

⅓ cup (75 mL) cane sugar

Sea salt

DIRECTIONS

In advance, make sure the freezer bowl of your ice-cream maker has been in the freezer overnight, or for at least 15 hours.

Remove the coconut milk from the fridge and carefully scoop the thick solid cream off the top. Save the watery part for another use (like the coconut cilantro chutney on page 195).

In a blender, combine the blueberries, mango, mint leaves, coconut solids, cornstarch, sugar, and a pinch of salt and puree until smooth.

Pour the mixture into the freezer bowl of your ice-cream maker and churn according to the manufacturer's directions.

Transfer to a freezer-safe container and chill for about 2 hours, or until the ice cream firms up. Serve!

If freezing overnight, let the ice cream soften at room temperature for about 20 minutes before serving.

VEGAN | **GLUTEN-FREE**

SERVES: 4

RASPBERRY LEMON DUTCH BABY

INGREDIENTS

DIRECTIONS

2 large eggs, at room temperature

½ cup (125 mL) almond milk, at room temperature

Pinch of sea salt

Pinch of cinnamon

½ cup (125 mL) all-purpose flour

3 tablespoons (45 mL) coconut oil, melted

¼ cup (60 mL) powdered sugar, sifted

Fresh lemon juice

½ cup (125 mL) raspberries

Preheat the oven to 425°F (215°C) with a 10-inch (25-cm) cast-iron skillet inside.

In a medium bowl, whisk together the eggs, almond milk, salt, and cinnamon until light and frothy. Gradually add the flour and whisk until just combined.

Using a pot holder, remove the preheated skillet from the oven and add the melted coconut oil, brushing to coat the bottom and sides of the pan. Pour the batter into the center of the hot pan.

Return the pan to the oven and bake until the edges are browned and the center is puffed up, 12 to 15 minutes.

Remove from the oven and serve immediately with the powdered sugar, a few squeezes of lemon juice, and the raspberries.

SERVES: **2** *OR* **3**

Most Dutch baby recipes use lots of butter and cream.
Ours is a slightly lighter version that uses coconut oil and almond milk,
but it tastes every bit as indulgent.

6

BROCCOLI

If you asked me when I was ten years old what my least favorite
food was, I would have said one thing without hesitation:
broccoli. My loathe turned to love the day I stopped preparing it
in the microwave. There's nothing better than the simplicity of
roasting it with a slight char, or cooking it with garlic and olive
oil in a skillet and serving it with pasta.

SEASON

FALL / WINTER

LEMON BROCCOLI & CAPER COUSCOUS

4 cups (1 L) broccoli florets

1½ cups (375 mL) cooked chickpeas, drained and rinsed (page 285)

Extra-virgin olive oil, for drizzling

1 cup (250 mL) dry Israeli couscous

1 tablespoon (15 mL) capers

¼ cup (60 mL) walnuts, toasted (page 285)

¼ teaspoon (1 mL) red pepper flakes

Sea salt and freshly ground black pepper

¼ cup (60 mL) grated pecorino cheese (optional)

- -

CHOPPED PESTO

½ cup (125 mL) fresh basil

¼ cup (60 mL) walnuts, toasted (page 285)

1 small garlic clove

2 to 3 tablespoons (30 to 45 mL) extra-virgin olive oil

2 tablespoons (30 mL) fresh lemon juice

1 teaspoon (5 mL) lemon zest

Sea salt and freshly ground black pepper

Yield: ½ cup (125 mL)

Preheat the oven to 400°F (200°C).

Line two baking sheets with parchment paper. Place the broccoli on one baking sheet and the chickpeas on the other. Drizzle the broccoli and chickpeas with olive oil and pinches of salt and pepper and toss. Roast for 20 minutes, or until the broccoli is browned around the edges.

Bring a medium pot of salted water to a boil. Prepare the couscous according to the instructions on the package, cooking until al dente, about 9 minutes.

Make the chopped pesto: On your cutting board, combine the basil, walnuts, and garlic. Finely chop the ingredients together, and then place the mixture in a small bowl. Stir in the olive oil, lemon juice, and lemon zest and season with salt and pepper.

Toss the couscous with the roasted chickpeas and broccoli and the capers, walnuts, red pepper flakes, and half of the pesto. Taste and adjust the seasonings, adding more salt, pepper, or pesto. Serve with the grated pecorino cheese, if using, and the extra pesto on the side.

VEGAN: Skip the cheese. | **GLUTEN-FREE:** Use quinoa or millet instead of couscous. | *SERVES:* **4**

While I hated broccoli as a kid, I loved my mom's cream of broccoli soup. This is a dairy-free version using coconut milk instead of milk or cream.

CREAMY BROCCOLI SOUP

DIRECTIONS

1 large leek

1 tablespoon (15 mL) extra-virgin olive oil, plus extra for garnish

2 garlic cloves, crushed

1 medium head broccoli

1½ teaspoons (7 mL) white wine vinegar

2 cups (500 mL) vegetable broth

1 cup (250 mL) light coconut milk, plus ¼ cup (60 mL) extra for garnish

2 to 3 cups (500 to 750 mL) loosely packed amaranth greens or spinach

Sea salt and freshly ground black pepper

Juice of 1 small lemon (optional)

Red pepper flakes (optional)

Slice the white and light green parts of the leek into rings. Using a strainer, rinse the leeks thoroughly.

Heat the olive oil in a large pot over medium heat. Add the leek, garlic, and a few generous pinches of salt and pepper. Stir and cook until the leek is soft, about 5 minutes.

Chop the broccoli, stems and all, into coarse florets and add them to the pot. Stir and cook until just softened, about 3 minutes.

Stir in the white wine vinegar, then add the vegetable broth and coconut milk. Reduce the heat to low and simmer for 5 minutes.

Let the soup cool slightly, then transfer to a blender (you can work in batches if you need to). Blend until smooth. Add the amaranth greens and blend again. Taste and adjust the seasonings, adding a bit of lemon juice to brighten it up a bit if you like.

Garnish with a drizzle of coconut milk and olive oil. Sprinkle with red pepper flakes, if desired.

VEGAN | **GLUTEN-FREE**

SERVES: **3** *OR* **4**

SWEET CHILI
CHARRED BROCCOLINI

DIRECTIONS

1 tablespoon (15 mL) tamari

2 small garlic cloves, minced

2 teaspoons (10 mL) rice vinegar

2 teaspoons (10 mL) cane sugar

½ teaspoon (2 mL) sriracha

Pinch of red pepper flakes

2 bunches of broccolini florets
(5 to 6 cups/1.25 to 1.5 L)

Preheat the oven to 400°F (200°C) and line
a baking sheet with parchment paper.

In a small bowl, whisk together the tamari,
minced garlic, rice vinegar, sugar, sriracha,
and red pepper flakes.

Place the broccolini on the baking sheet
and toss with half of the sauce, then
spread the broccolini evenly so that the
pieces are not touching each other. Roast
for 15 minutes, or until the broccolini
is charred on the edges. Serve with the
remaining sauce on the side for dipping.

TIP The chili glaze is delicious with other vegetables, too. Try it with roasted
brussels sprouts, sweet potatoes, or eggplant.

VEGAN | **GLUTEN-FREE**

SERVES: **4** *AS AN APPETIZER*

TIP:

No broccoli rabe? Sub in
kale or Swiss chard.

BROCCOLI RABE
& SUNCHOKE ORECCHIETTE

INGREDIENTS	DIRECTIONS
2 tablespoons (30 mL) extra-virgin olive oil, plus extra for drizzling	In a large skillet, heat the olive oil over medium heat. Add the sunchokes and season with salt and pepper. Cook in a thin layer until both sides are browned, about 2 minutes per side. Remove from the skillet and drain on a paper towel.
5 sunchokes, sliced into ¼-inch (0.5-cm) slices	
8 ounces (225 g) orecchiette pasta	
1 shallot, chopped	Meanwhile, bring a large pot of salted water to a boil. Prepare the pasta according to the instructions on the package, cooking until al dente. Drain the pasta.
1 garlic clove, minced	
3 cups (750 mL) chopped broccoli rabe	
2 tablespoons (30 mL) fresh lemon juice	Wipe any excess oil from the skillet and drizzle enough olive oil to lightly coat the bottom of the pan. Add the shallot and cook until soft, about 2 minutes. Add the garlic, broccoli rabe, and lemon juice. Season with salt and pepper. Toss until the broccoli rabe wilts, about 2 minutes. Add the cooked pasta, sunchokes, lemon zest, feta cheese, pine nuts, red pepper flakes, and a grating of the pecorino cheese, if desired. Taste and adjust the seasonings.
1 teaspoon (5 mL) lemon zest	
¼ cup (60 mL) crumbled feta cheese	
¼ cup (60 mL) pine nuts	
Pinch of red pepper flakes	
Sea salt and freshly ground black pepper	
Grated pecorino cheese (optional)	

VEGAN: Skip the cheese.

GLUTEN-FREE: Use gluten-free pasta (another shape, if necessary).

SERVES: 4

BRUSSELS

7

S P R O U T S

{ My favorite thing about food trends is how the most hated vegetable can suddenly become the most loved. I didn't grow up eating brussels sprouts, but once they started showing up on restaurant menus, I couldn't get enough. Cooking with them at home made me realize that they're so incredibly versatile! Roast them in the oven and finish with a squeeze of lemon juice, char them in a skillet and toss them into creamy pastas, or shred them into salads. If you can find brussels sprouts that are still on their stalk, use their larger leaves to make lettuce wraps (page 71). }

SEASON

FALL / WINTER

TIP :: Asparagus, broccoli, shiitake mushrooms, red bell peppers, and roasted butternut squash are all delicious in here as well.

COCONUT RICE
WITH BRUSSELS SPROUTS

1 cup (250 mL) jasmine rice

1¼ cups (300 mL) canned light coconut milk

2 teaspoons (10 mL) coconut oil

2 cups (500 mL) brussels sprouts, sliced in half

Pinch of sea salt

¼ cup (60 mL) chopped scallions

¼ cup (60 mL) torn basil

¼ cup (60 mL) torn mint

1 small avocado, pitted and diced

1 tablespoon (15 mL) sesame seeds

Sriracha

Lime slices, for serving

- -

SAUCE

1 tablespoon (15 mL) tamari

2 small garlic cloves, minced

2 teaspoons (10 mL) fresh lime juice

2 teaspoons (10 mL) rice vinegar

1 tablespoon (15 mL) cane sugar

2 tablespoons (30 mL) water

2 Thai chilies, diced, or ½ teaspoon (2 mL) red pepper flakes

Cook the rice according to the instructions on page 284, using coconut milk instead of water. Alternatively, cook the rice in a rice cooker according to the manufacturer's directions for white rice, but use coconut milk in place of water. Fluff with a fork and keep warm.

Make the sauce: In a small bowl, whisk together the tamari, minced garlic, lime juice, rice vinegar, sugar, water, and chilies. Set aside.

Heat the coconut oil in a large skillet over medium-high heat. Add the brussels sprouts, cut side down, along with the salt. Let them sear until the cut side becomes golden brown, 2 to 3 minutes. Toss and continue cooking for an additional 7 to 10 minutes, or until tender.

Add the scallions during the last 2 minutes of cooking. Remove from the heat.

Serve the rice in bowls with the brussels sprouts, sauce, basil, mint, avocado, and sesame seeds. Serve with sriracha and lime slices on the side.

VEGAN | **GLUTEN-FREE**

SERVES: **4**

CREAMY MISO BRUSSELS SPROUT FETTUCCINE

INGREDIENTS

DIRECTIONS

SAUCE

½ cup (125 mL) raw cashews, soaked
3 to 4 hours, preferably overnight, drained,
and rinsed

1 tablespoon (15 mL) white miso paste

1 small garlic clove

¼ teaspoon (1 mL) Dijon mustard

½ cup (125 mL) fresh water

2 tablespoons (30 mL) fresh lemon juice

1 tablespoon (15 mL) extra-virgin olive oil

Sea salt

- -

1 teaspoon (5 mL) extra-virgin olive oil

2 cups (500 mL) brussels sprouts,
sliced in half

1 teaspoon (5 mL) fresh lemon juice

8 ounces (225 g) fettuccine

Sea salt and freshly ground black pepper

Make the sauce: In a high-speed blender,
puree the cashews, miso paste, garlic,
Dijon mustard, water, lemon juice, olive
oil, and a pinch of salt until smooth. Taste
and adjust the seasonings.

Heat the oil in a large skillet over medium-
high heat. Add the brussels sprouts, cut
side down, along with a pinch of salt.
Let them sear until the cut side becomes
golden brown, 2 to 3 minutes. Toss and
continue cooking for an additional 7 to
10 minutes, or until tender.

Add a squeeze of lemon juice to the pan,
toss once more, then remove from the heat
and transfer to a plate.

Bring a large pot of salted water to a
boil. Prepare the pasta according to the
instructions on the package, cooking until
al dente. Reserve 1 cup (250 mL) of the
pasta water. Drain and return the pasta
to the pot. Stir in the sauce, adding pasta
water as needed to thin the sauce and
make it creamy. Add the brussels sprouts
and toss until heated through.

NOTE If you're using a traditional blender, not a Vitamix or other high-speed blender,
you may need to blend an additional minute, or until the sauce is creamy.

VEGAN | **GLUTEN-FREE:** Use brown rice fettuccine. | *SERVES:* **3** *OR* **4**

BRUSSELS SPROUT
BREAKFAST TOSTADAS

4 corn tortillas

Extra-virgin olive oil, for brushing and drizzling

8 to 10 brussels sprouts, sliced

4 large eggs

1 small avocado

Juice of ½ lime

¼ cup (60 mL) cooked black beans, drained and rinsed (page 285)

2 radishes, sliced

Sea salt and freshly ground black pepper

Hot sauce (optional)

Brush the tortillas with olive oil and toast in a cast-iron skillet over medium-high heat for 2 to 3 minutes per side, or until crispy. Or bake in the oven at 300°F (150°C) for 10 to 15 minutes, or until crispy. Remove and set aside.

Add a drizzle of olive oil to the skillet and place the shredded brussels sprouts in a thin layer with a pinch of salt and pepper. Use tongs to flip the shredded brussels sprouts as they brown. Remove them from the pan once they're lightly golden brown, about 4 minutes.

In a nonstick skillet, fry the eggs until the whites are set and the yolks are still runny.

Use the back of a fork to smash a quarter of the avocado onto each tortilla and add a squeeze of lime juice and a pinch of salt. Assemble each tortilla with the brussels sprouts, black beans, eggs, radishes, and pepper. Serve with hot sauce, if desired.

GLUTEN-FREE

SERVES: **4**

SHREDDED BRUSSELS SPROUT & CRANBERRY SALAD

INGREDIENTS

4 cups (1 L) brussels sprouts

¼ cup (60 mL) extra-virgin olive oil, plus extra for drizzling

¼ cup (60 mL) fresh lemon juice

½ cup (125 mL) pine nuts, toasted (page 285)

⅓ cup (75 mL) dried cranberries

⅓ cup (75 mL) grated pecorino cheese

⅓ cup (75 mL) chopped chives

Sea salt and freshly ground black pepper

DIRECTIONS

Thinly slice the brussels sprouts using a mandoline if you have one. Place them into a medium bowl and toss with the olive oil, lemon juice, pine nuts, cranberries, pecorino cheese, chives, and pinches of salt and pepper.

Let the salad sit at room temperature for 15 minutes, then taste and adjust the seasonings. Finish with an additional drizzle of olive oil if you like.

VEGAN: Skip the cheese. | **GLUTEN-FREE** | *SERVES:* **4** *AS A SIDE*

In the fall when I've been getting a little too cozy with comfort food, I like to make this salad to lighten things up. Because the brussels sprouts are raw, find the best ones you can. This salad is pretty basic, but I like to make variations by adding shaved apple, shaved fennel, or torn kale pieces, just to name a few.

BRUSSELS SPROUT WRAPS WITH ALMOND SAUCE

7 ounces (200 g) extra-firm tofu

Coconut oil, for drizzling

Tamari, for drizzling

4 ounces (125 g) pad thai or vermicelli rice noodles

8 brussels sprout leaves from the stalks or lettuce cups

1 carrot, peeled into ribbons

¼ cup (60 mL) sliced almonds

1 recipe peanut sauce (page 286), substituting almond butter for peanut butter

Lime slices

Sea salt and freshly ground black pepper

1 serrano pepper, sliced (optional)

Sriracha (optional)

DIRECTIONS

Slice the tofu into 1-inch (2.5-cm)-thick planks. Pat dry, then drizzle with coconut oil, tamari, and pinches of salt and pepper.

Add a drizzle of coconut oil to a small skillet and heat over medium-high heat. Sear each side of the tofu until golden brown, about 4 minutes per side. Remove and slice into thin strips.

Prepare the rice noodles according to the instructions on the package.

Assemble the wraps on the brussels sprout leaves with the tofu, noodles, carrots, and almonds. Serve with the almond sauce, lime slices, and serrano slices and sriracha, if using.

TIP Look for brussels sprouts that are still attached to their stalk and use the greens to make these wraps. If you can't find one, use Bibb or butter lettuce instead.

VEGAN | **GLUTEN-FREE**

SERVES: **4**

8

CABBAGE& CHICORIES

For me, cabbage is an acquired taste that I've only learned to appreciate somewhat recently. That is, except for mayonnaise- and sugar-laden coleslaws, which I have an extreme weakness for. I enjoy the bitter bite of it (and its chicory friends) in very simple ways—red cabbage with a squeeze of lime topped onto sandwiches or tacos, radicchio leaves to hold a quinoa filling, and crispy endive spears as a healthier way to scoop hummus.

SEASON

WINTER / VARIES

QUINOA SALAD RADICCHIO CUPS

DRESSING

2 tablespoons (30 mL) extra-virgin olive oil

2 tablespoons (30 mL) fresh lemon juice

2 tablespoons (30 mL) fresh orange juice

1 teaspoon (5 mL) Dijon mustard

1 garlic clove, minced

Sea salt and freshly ground black pepper

- -

1½ cups (375 mL) cooked quinoa (page 284)

½ cup (125 mL) sliced cherry tomatoes

½ cup (125 mL) chopped cucumber

¼ cup (60 mL) crumbled feta cheese

¼ cup (60 mL) pine nuts

2 tablespoons (30 mL) chopped chives

1 small head radicchio, separated into
8 leaves

Sea salt and freshly ground black pepper

Make the dressing: In a small bowl, whisk together the olive oil, lemon juice, orange juice, Dijon mustard, and garlic. Season with salt and pepper.

Toss the dressing with the cooked quinoa, cherry tomatoes, cucumber, feta cheese, pine nuts, and chives. Taste and adjust the seasonings. The salad should taste sweet, tangy, and slightly overdressed, which will help balance the bitter flavor of the radicchio.

Fill the radicchio leaves with the quinoa filling and serve.

The quinoa filling can be made up to 1 day in advance and stored in the fridge.

TIP The quinoa salad is good on its own, too—make it the night before and pack it up for lunch the next day!

VEGAN: Skip the cheese. | **GLUTEN-FREE** | *SERVES:* **4** *AS AN APPETIZER*

ASIAN CHOPPED CABBAGE SALAD

5 cups (1.25 L) thinly shaved red or green cabbage

1 cup (250 mL) small broccoli florets

1 carrot, thinly sliced

2 radishes, sliced into matchsticks

3 satsumas or small oranges, sliced into segments

8 ounces (225 g) extra-firm tofu, cut into small cubes

1 small avocado, pitted and diced

⅓ cup (75 mL) crushed peanuts, toasted (page 285)

2 teaspoons (10 mL) sesame seeds

PEANUT DRESSING

¼ cup (60 mL) creamy peanut butter

1½ tablespoons (22 mL) toasted sesame oil

2 teaspoons (10 mL) tamari, plus extra if desired

⅓ cup (75 mL) fresh satsuma juice

1 tablespoon (15 mL) rice vinegar

1 teaspoon (5 mL) freshly grated ginger

1 teaspoon (5 mL) sriracha, plus extra if desired

2 tablespoons (30 mL) water

In a large bowl, toss the shaved cabbage together with the broccoli, carrot, radishes, satsuma segments, tofu, and avocado.

Make the peanut dressing: In a small bowl, whisk together the peanut butter, sesame oil, tamari, satsuma juice, rice vinegar, ginger, sriracha, and water.

Pour the sauce over the salad and toss. Chill for 20 minutes. Season to taste with more tamari as desired.

Top with the toasted peanuts and sesame seeds.

Serve with extra sriracha on the side.

VEGAN | **GLUTEN-FREE** *SERVES:* **4**

ENDIVE WITH SWEET PEA AVOCADO HUMMUS

INGREDIENTS

1½ cups (375 mL) cooked chickpeas, drained and rinsed (page 285)

½ cup (125 mL) peas (blanched 1 minute if fresh; thawed if frozen)

1 small avocado

1 garlic clove

Juice and zest of 1 small lemon

¼ teaspoon (1 mL) cumin

3 tablespoons (45 mL) extra-virgin olive oil

Spears from 2 Belgian endives

Sea salt and freshly ground black pepper

2 pitas, toasted and sliced (optional)

DIRECTIONS

Place the chickpeas, peas, avocado, garlic, lemon juice, lemon zest, and cumin in a food processor. Pulse until well combined. Add the olive oil and season with salt and pepper. Pulse until smooth. Serve with endive spears and toasted pita, if desired.

Store extra hummus in the refrigerator for 1 day.

VEGAN | **GLUTEN-FREE**

SERVES: **4**

BALSAMIC GRILLED
RADICCHIO SALAD

INGREDIENTS

2 small heads radicchio

Extra-virgin olive oil, for drizzling

White balsamic vinegar, for drizzling

2 cups (500 mL) mixed salad greens

⅓ cup (75 mL) hazelnuts,
chopped and toasted (page 285)

Parmesan cheese wedge, for shaving

Sea salt and freshly ground black pepper

2 slices grainy bread (optional)

½ garlic clove (optional)

DIRECTIONS

Preheat a grill or grill pan to medium heat.

Slice the radicchio into wedges and drizzle
with olive oil, white balsamic vinegar, and
pinches of salt and pepper. Grill each side
for about 3 minutes, or until char marks
form and the radicchio softens.

Remove from the grill and assemble the
radicchio wedges on plates with a small
handful of salad greens. Drizzle with olive
oil and a little bit of balsamic vinegar. Top
with the toasted hazelnuts and shavings
of Parmesan cheese. Serve with freshly
ground black pepper.

If desired, make toasted bread crumbs:
Toast 2 slices of grainy bread until crispy.
Rub with the cut side of the garlic clove.
In a food processor, pulse the bread into
coarse crumbs. Sprinkle on the salads.

GLUTEN-FREE: Skip the croutons.

SERVES: **4**

1 Pulse the chickpea salad ingredients together in a food processor.

2 Chop the fixins—cabbage, radishes, lettuce, and basil.

3 Build your sandwich.

4 Dig in!

CHICKPEA SALAD SANDWICH WITH CRUNCHY RED CABBAGE

CHICKPEA SALAD

1½ cups (375 mL) cooked chickpeas, drained and rinsed (page 285)

1 teaspoon (5 mL) Dijon mustard

2 tablespoons (30 mL) tahini

½ garlic clove

1 teaspoon (5 mL) capers

1 scallion, chopped

¼ cup (60 mL) chopped cilantro

Juice of 1 small lemon (save a few squeezes for the cabbage topping)

Sea salt and freshly ground black pepper

- -

1 cup (250 mL) shredded cabbage

Slices of soft whole-grain bread

Mayonnaise

Radishes, thinly sliced

Arugula or lettuce

Basil

Make the chickpea salad: Combine the chickpeas, Dijon mustard, tahini, garlic, capers, scallion, cilantro, lemon juice, and pinches of salt and pepper. Mash with a potato masher, or pulse in a food processor, until cohesive yet still chunky. Chill until ready to use.

In a small bowl, mix the shredded cabbage with a squeeze of lemon and a pinch of salt. Chill for 5 minutes.

Assemble the sandwiches with whole-grain bread, a slather of mayonnaise, the chickpea salad, cabbage, sliced radishes, arugula, and basil.

VEGAN: Use vegan mayonnaise.

GLUTEN-FREE: Use gluten-free bread.

SERVES: **2** *TO* **4**

TIP: Don't toss those vibrant tops—blend them into pesto or chop them finely and toss them into your salad.

9

CARROTS

The best way to become a carrot lover: Step away from the bagged baby carrots. There's nothing baby about them—they're just large fibrous carrots that get whittled down. Instead, head to your farmers market and look for the smaller heirloom varieties that are sweet, tender, and crispy.

SEASON

SPRING / FALL

VEGAN CARROT WAFFLES

2 cups (500 mL) whole spelt flour or white/wheat mix

2 teaspoons (10 mL) baking powder

2 tablespoons (30 mL) ground flaxseed

½ teaspoon (2 mL) cinnamon

1 cup (250 mL) grated carrots

2 cups (500 mL) almond milk at room temperature

¼ cup (60 mL) melted coconut oil

1 teaspoon (5 mL) vanilla extract

2 tablespoons (30 mL) maple syrup, plus extra for serving

Sea salt

1 recipe coconut cream (page 287) (optional)

Preheat a waffle iron.

In a large bowl, mix the flour, baking powder, flaxseed, cinnamon, and a pinch of salt.

In a medium bowl, mix together the grated carrots, almond milk, coconut oil, vanilla, and maple syrup. Fold the carrot mixture into the dry ingredients and stir until just combined.

Scoop an appropriate amount of batter onto your waffle iron and cook until the edges are slightly crisp. Serve with maple syrup and the coconut cream, if using.

Yield: 4 to 6 waffles

VEGAN

SERVES: **4**

Love cold soups
as much as I do?
Here's a carrot
gazpacho that'll
make you forget
that gazpacho
is supposed to
have tomatoes.

CARROT GAZPACHO
WITH LEMONGRASS

1 stalk lemongrass

16 ounces (450 g) peak-season carrots, peeled and sliced, about 2 bunches

1 (14-ounce/414-mL) can light or full-fat coconut milk; reserve ¼ cup for garnish

1 garlic clove

2 tablespoons (30 mL) extra-virgin olive oil, plus more for drizzling

2 tablespoons (30 mL) sherry vinegar

1 teaspoon (5 mL) red curry paste

½ cup (125 mL) filtered water

Sea salt and freshly ground black pepper

Optional garnishes: hemp seeds, pepitas, microgreens, drizzles of coconut milk

Prepare the lemongrass by cutting off the root end and the tough upper stem of the stalk. Remove the first one or two layers of outer leaves and finely chop the tender, aromatic part of the lemongrass.

Using a high-speed blender, combine the lemongrass, carrots, coconut milk, garlic, olive oil, sherry vinegar, red curry paste, water, and a few generous pinches of salt and pepper. Blend until smooth. If you're not using a high-speed blender like a Vitamix, strain the soup and blend again until completely smooth.

Chill for at least 4 hours. If the soup thickens in the fridge, stir in a little more cold water. Add more salt and pepper, to taste.

Drizzle with olive oil and serve with desired garnishes.

VEGAN | **GLUTEN-FREE**

SERVES: **4**

CARROT RIBBON TACOS

1½ cups (375 mL) cooked chickpeas, drained and rinsed (page 285)

Extra-virgin olive oil, for drizzling

½ garlic clove, minced

¼ teaspoon (1 mL) cumin

4 medium carrots

8 corn tortillas, grilled or warmed

1 mango, peeled and cubed

3 radishes, thinly sliced

Few handfuls of cilantro leaves, stems reserved

Sriracha, for serving

Sea salt and freshly ground black pepper

1 serrano pepper, thinly sliced (optional)

CILANTRO-STEM YOGURT SAUCE

7 ounces (200 g) Greek yogurt

⅔ cup (150 mL) reserved cilantro stems

2 scallions, chopped

½ garlic clove

½ teaspoon (2 mL) dried coriander

Juice of 1 lime

1 tablespoon + 1 teaspoon (20 mL) olive oil

Sea salt and freshly ground black pepper

½ teaspoon (2 mL) honey (optional)

Preheat the broiler of your oven, and line a baking sheet with parchment paper.

Toss the chickpeas with a drizzle of olive oil, garlic, cumin, and pinches of salt and pepper. Broil for 3 to 5 minutes, or until the chickpeas are slightly golden brown.

Peel the carrots into ribbons and set aside.

Make the cilantro-stem yogurt sauce: In a food processor, pulse the yogurt, cilantro stems, scallions, garlic, coriander, lime juice, and pinches of salt and pepper. With the food processor running, drizzle in the olive oil. Taste and adjust the seasonings. If it's too tart, add a bit of honey if you'd like. Chill until ready to use.

Fill each tortilla with the yogurt sauce, chickpeas, mango, radishes, carrot ribbons, cilantro, and serrano pepper, if using.

Serve with the sriracha on the side.

VEGAN: Make the yogurt sauce with sun "cheese" (page 286) and skip the honey.

GLUTEN-FREE

SERVES: **4**

CARROT-GINGER GRAIN BOWL

INGREDIENTS

10 small heirloom carrots

8 ounces (225 g) extra-firm tofu,
cut into cubes

Extra-virgin olive oil, for drizzling

½ teaspoon (2 mL) sriracha

2 cups (500 mL) mixed greens

2 cups (500 mL) cooked millet (page 284)

¼ cup (60 mL) chopped carrot greens

⅓ cup (75 mL) chopped almonds

1 recipe carrot-ginger sauce (page 287)

1 small avocado, diced

Sea salt and freshly ground black pepper

DIRECTIONS

Preheat the oven to 400°F (200°C).

Use a vegetable peeler to peel 3 carrots into ribbons. Save any leftover carrot pieces for roasting.

Line two baking sheets with parchment paper. Cut the remaining 7 carrots vertically in quarters and arrange on the first baking sheet along with any leftover carrot pieces. Place the tofu cubes on the second baking sheet. Toss the carrots and tofu cubes with a drizzle of olive oil, and season with salt and pepper. Bake for 15 to 17 minutes, or until golden brown around the edges. The carrots should still have some bite to them.

Remove the tofu from the oven, toss it lightly with sriracha, and return it to the oven for 2 more minutes.

Toss the salad greens with the cooked millet, carrot greens, almonds, a third of the carrot-ginger sauce, and a few pinches of salt.

Assemble the bowls with the millet salad, roasted carrots, carrot ribbons, tofu, avocado, and pepper. Serve with the remaining carrot-ginger sauce on the side.

VEGAN: Skip the honey. | **GLUTEN-FREE** | *SERVES:* **4**

CARROT & TOMATO TAGLIATELLE

INGREDIENTS

1 tablespoon (15 mL) extra-virgin olive oil

1 medium shallot, chopped

1½ cups (375 mL) chopped carrots

3 garlic cloves, minced

1 teaspoon (5 mL) dried oregano

¼ teaspoon (1 mL) red pepper flakes

¼ cup (60 mL) dry white wine

1 tablespoon (15 mL) balsamic vinegar

1 can (14.5 ounces/411 g) diced tomatoes

4 ounces (125 g) tagliatelle pasta

2 cups (500 mL) chopped kale leaves

½ cup (125 mL) cooked cannellini beans, drained and rinsed (page 285)

¼ cup (60 mL) pine nuts

2 teaspoons (10 mL) capers

Chopped chives or other herbs (basil, parsley, etc.)

Sea salt and freshly ground black pepper

Grated Parmesan cheese (optional)

DIRECTIONS

In a large pot, heat the olive oil over medium heat. Add the shallot and a pinch of salt and pepper and cook until soft, about 2 minutes. Add the carrots, garlic, oregano, red pepper flakes, and another few pinches of salt. Let cook, stirring occasionally, until the vegetables are lightly browned, about 5 minutes.

Add the white wine. Stir and let the wine cook off until it's nearly evaporated, about 30 seconds. Add the balsamic vinegar and tomatoes. Cover and reduce the heat to a simmer. Cook until the carrots are tender, about 15 minutes.

Meanwhile, bring a medium pot of salted water to a boil. Prepare the pasta according to the instructions on the package, cooking until al dente. Drain the pasta.

Stir the chopped kale into the sauce and let it wilt down, about 1 minute. Add the pasta, cannellini beans, pine nuts, capers, and chives or herbs. Season with salt and pepper to taste and serve with freshly grated Parmesan cheese, if desired.

VEGAN: Use fettuccine or linguine noodles.

GLUTEN-FREE: Use brown rice tagliatelle.

SERVES: 4

10

CAULIFLOWER

The most versatile vegetable of them all! Here are my two favorite ways to use cauliflower:

PUREED

Puree into soups or sauces, or try mixing cauliflower puree into your mashed potatoes for a lighter take on the traditional Thanksgiving side.

ROASTED

Roast the florets until they're golden brown. Then put them on anything from pizza (page 105) to tacos (page 99). Very often, I'll just eat the roasted cauliflower hot off the baking sheet and call it dinner.

SEASON

WINTER

ROASTED CAULIFLOWER TACOS WITH CHIPOTLE CREAM

1 medium head cauliflower, cut into small florets

Extra-virgin olive oil, for drizzling

2 chipotle peppers from canned chipotles in adobo sauce

8 tortillas, warmed or grilled

1 medium avocado, sliced

Cilantro

1 lime, sliced

Sea salt and freshly ground black pepper

CHIPOTLE YOGURT SAUCE

7 ounces (200 g) full-fat Greek yogurt

1 chipotle pepper (from the can used above)

1 small garlic clove

1 teaspoon (5 mL) fresh lime juice, plus more to taste

1 teaspoon (5 mL) extra-virgin olive oil

1 teaspoon (5 mL) honey

Sea salt and freshly ground black pepper

Preheat the oven to 400°F (200°C).

Line a large baking sheet with parchment paper. Add the cauliflower and drizzle with olive oil and a pinch of salt and pepper. Toss to combine. Working over the baking sheet, use your hands to break up 2 chipotle peppers, along with some of the adobo sauce. Toss again to coat the cauliflower and roast for 25 to 30 minutes, or until golden brown.

Make the chipotle yogurt sauce: In a small food processor, combine the yogurt, chipotle pepper, garlic, lime juice, olive oil, honey, and a pinch of salt. Blend until smooth. Taste and adjust the seasonings, adding more salt, pepper, and lime juice as desired.

Fill each tortilla with a spoonful of sauce, the roasted cauliflower, and a slice of avocado. Serve with the cilantro and lime slices on the side.

VEGAN: Make the chipotle sauce with sun "cheese" (page 286) and skip the honey.

GLUTEN-FREE

SERVES: **4**

ROASTED CAULIFLOWER & RED PEPPER SOUP

1 small head cauliflower, cut into florets

1 small yellow onion, sliced

3 garlic cloves, unpeeled

Extra-virgin olive oil, for drizzling

½ cup (125 mL) raw unsalted cashews, soaked 3 to 4 hours, preferably overnight

3 tablespoons (45 mL) white miso paste

3 cups (750 mL) water

½ teaspoon (2 mL) cumin

½ teaspoon (2 mL) coriander

Pinch of cayenne pepper

3 roasted red bell peppers, fresh or from a jar

Sea salt and freshly ground black pepper

1 teaspoon (5 mL) sherry vinegar or white wine vinegar (optional)

Preheat the oven to 400°F (200°C).

Line two baking sheets with parchment paper. Fill one sheet with the cauliflower florets and the other with the sliced onion and garlic cloves. Drizzle both sheets with olive oil, season with salt and pepper, and toss to combine. Roast 20 to 30 minutes, until golden brown. Check at 20 minutes, as the onion might roast faster than the cauliflower. Reserve 1 cup (250 mL) of the roasted florets for garnish.

Drain and rinse the cashews and place them in a high-speed blender. Peel the roasted garlic cloves and add them to the blender with the cauliflower, onion, miso paste, fresh water, cumin, coriander, cayenne pepper, and roasted red bell peppers. Blend until creamy. Season with salt and pepper to taste. For extra brightness, add a splash of sherry vinegar or white wine vinegar.

Garnish with a drizzle of olive oil and the reserved roasted cauliflower.

VEGAN | GLUTEN-FREE

SERVES: **4**

CURRIED CAULIFLOWER FRIED RICE

INGREDIENTS

1½ cups (375 mL) cooked basmati rice (page 284)

1 tablespoon (15 mL) coconut oil

2 medium shallots, chopped

2 to 3 cups (500 to 750 mL) cauliflower florets, crumbled into small pieces

⅓ cup (75 mL) raw unsalted cashews

½ cup (125 mL) cooked chickpeas, drained and rinsed (page 285)

1 teaspoon (5 mL) curry powder

½ teaspoon (2 mL) turmeric

¼ teaspoon (1 mL) red pepper flakes

¼ cup (60 mL) chopped scallions

¾ cup (175 mL) canned full-fat or light coconut milk

2 teaspoons (10 mL) fresh lime juice

¼ cup (60 mL) currants

¼ cup (60 mL) chopped mint

Sea salt and freshly ground black pepper

CARDAMOM YOGURT SAUCE

½ cup (125 mL) Greek yogurt

Juice of ½ lime

¼ teaspoon (1 mL) ground cardamom

Sea salt and freshly ground black pepper

DIRECTIONS

Cook the rice according to the directions on page 284. Set aside.

Make the cardamom yogurt sauce: In a small bowl, combine the yogurt, lime juice, cardamom, and a pinch of salt and pepper. Chill until ready to serve.

In a large skillet, heat the coconut oil over medium heat. Add the shallots, cauliflower, and pinches of salt and pepper. Cook until the cauliflower is lightly browned, about 5 minutes. Add the cashews and chickpeas and cook until lightly browned, about 5 more minutes.

Add the curry powder, turmeric, red pepper flakes, and scallions. Stir and cook until the spices are fragrant, about 30 seconds. Reduce the heat and add ½ cup (125 mL) of the coconut milk. Then add the lime juice, currants, and another pinch of salt. Add the rice and stir to incorporate, breaking up any clumpy rice grains. Add the remaining ¼ cup (60 mL) coconut milk and stir in the mint. Season to taste.

Serve with the cardamom yogurt sauce.

VEGAN: Skip the cardamom yogurt sauce. | **GLUTEN-FREE** | *SERVES:* **4**

ROASTED CAULIFLOWER & PEAR PIZZA

INGREDIENTS

1 recipe homemade pizza dough (page 285)

1 small head of cauliflower, broken into very small florets, about 2 cups (500 mL)

Cornmeal, for sprinkling

Extra-virgin olive oil, for drizzling and brushing

1½ cups (375 mL) grated white cheddar cheese

1 unripe pear, thinly sliced

⅓ cup (75 mL) crumbled feta or gorgonzola cheese

¼ teaspoon (1 mL) red pepper flakes

Few handfuls of arugula

Sea salt and freshly ground black pepper

Honey, for drizzling (optional)

DIRECTIONS

Prepare the homemade pizza dough.

Preheat the oven to 400°F (200°C) and line a baking sheet with parchment paper. Place the cauliflower on the baking sheet and toss with a drizzle of olive oil and pinches of salt and pepper. Roast for 20 minutes, or until the cauliflower begins to turn golden brown.

On a lightly floured flat surface, roll the pizza dough into a 12-inch (30-cm) circle. Add flour as needed to prevent sticking. Place the pizza on a baking sheet sprinkled with cornmeal. Brush the dough with olive oil and bake for 5 minutes.

Remove the dough from the oven and top with half of the white cheddar cheese, the sliced pear, feta cheese, cauliflower, and the remaining white cheddar. Bake for an additional 15 to 20 minutes, or until the crust is golden brown and the cheese is melted. Remove from the oven. Top with the red pepper flakes and arugula. Drizzle with olive oil and honey, if desired.

SERVES: **2** *OR* **3**

Sometimes ideas come from unexpected places; I got the idea of "pearing" pears and cauliflower from a sushi roll I had at Uchi here in Austin. I love the sweet and savory combination of these two ingredients.

11

Citrus

You've probably noticed by now that I add a
squeeze of lemon to just about everything I make.
In the same way that salt enhances flavor, acidic
foods, such as lemons and limes, are essential to
create food that tastes bright and vibrant.

SEASON

WINTER

GRAPEFRUIT, QUINOA & FENNEL SALAD WITH MINT

INGREDIENTS

1 small fennel bulb, white part, thinly sliced

1 watermelon radish, thinly sliced

1½ teaspoons (7 mL) extra-virgin olive oil

1 tablespoon (15 mL) fresh lemon juice

½ teaspoon (2 mL) white wine vinegar

¼ teaspoon (1 mL) honey

½ cup (125 mL) grapefruit segments

2 cups (500 mL) mixed salad greens

½ cup (125 mL) cooked quinoa (page 284)

⅓ cup (75 mL) crumbled feta cheese

¼ cup (60 mL) pine nuts, toasted (page 285)

Small handful of mint leaves

Sea salt and freshly ground black pepper

DIRECTIONS

In a large bowl, combine the sliced fennel, watermelon radish, olive oil, lemon juice, white wine vinegar, honey, grapefruit segments, and a few pinches of salt and pepper.

Toss to combine, then add the salad greens, quinoa, feta cheese, pine nuts, and mint. Toss again. Season with salt and pepper to taste.

SERVES: 4 AS A SIDE OR 2 AS A MAIN

MINTY FRENCH 75

MINT SYRUP

1 cup (250 mL) cane sugar

1 cup (250 mL) water

½ cup (125 mL) loosely packed mint leaves, plus a few extra for garnish

Yield: Makes 1 cup. Extra can be stored in the refrigerator up to 1 month.

COCKTAIL

2 ounces (60 mL) gin

1 ounce (30 mL) mint syrup

1 ounce (30 mL) lemon juice

Crushed ice

2 ounces (60 mL) Prosecco

Make the mint syrup: In a small saucepan, bring the sugar and water to a boil. Reduce the heat and simmer, stirring until the sugar is dissolved, 1 to 2 minutes.

Remove from the heat and stir in the mint leaves. Let cool for 15 minutes. Strain and chill until ready to serve.

Make the cocktail by shaking the gin, mint syrup, lemon juice, and ice in a cocktail shaker. Pour into two glasses, add the Prosecco, and garnish with mint.

YIELD: MAKES **2** *COCKTAILS*

When I make cocktails at home, I keep them really simple and approach them like I would a meal—balanced, not too sweet, and finished with fresh herbs and a squeeze of lemon.

VEGGIE CEVICHE

CEVICHE

¼ cup (60 mL) finely diced red onion

1 scallion, finely chopped
(2 tablespoons/30 mL)

1 red bell pepper, stem and ribbing
removed and finely diced (1 cup/250 mL)

½ to 1 jalapeño pepper, finely diced

1 small Granny Smith apple, finely diced
(1 cup/250 mL)

1½ cups (375 mL) fresh corn kernels, cut
from about 2 ears of corn

3 tablespoons (45 mL) fresh orange juice

3 tablespoons (45 mL) fresh lime juice

½ teaspoon (2 mL) lime zest

½ cup (125 mL) chopped cilantro

Sea salt and freshly ground black pepper

- -

2 ripe plantains

Extra-virgin olive oil, for drizzling

Sea salt and freshly ground black pepper

Make the ceviche: In a medium bowl,
mix all of the ceviche ingredients
together. Chill for at least 20 minutes.
After chilling, season the ceviche with
additional salt to taste.

Preheat the oven to 400°F (200°C) and
line a baking sheet with parchment paper.

Slice off the ends of the plantains and
peel. Cut into thin, ¼-inch (0.5-cm) slices
on a bias. Arrange the plantain slices on
the baking sheet. Drizzle with olive oil
and pinches of salt and pepper. Bake for
20 minutes, then flip the plantains with
a spatula and bake for an additional
5 minutes.

Serve ceviche with the plantain slices. It
can also be served with tortilla chips.

VEGAN | **GLUTEN-FREE**

SERVES: **6** *AS AN APPETIZER*

BEET & CARROT SALAD WITH SWEET CITRUS VINAIGRETTE

INGREDIENTS

4 medium yellow beets, or any other color

2 tablespoons (30 mL) extra-virgin olive oil, plus more for drizzling

2 tablespoons (30 mL) fresh lemon juice, plus more to taste

2 tablespoons (30 mL) fresh orange juice

2 tablespoons (30 mL) white wine vinegar

1 teaspoon (5 mL) Dijon mustard

½ garlic clove, minced

4 red radishes, thinly sliced

4 medium carrots, peeled into thin strips

1 cup (250 mL) cooked farro or quinoa (page 284)

½ cup (125 mL) sliced fresh mint

2 cups baby salad greens

Sea salt and freshly ground black pepper

½ cup (125 mL) cooked chickpeas (page 284) (optional)

¼ cup (60 mL) crumbled feta cheese (optional)

DIRECTIONS

Preheat the oven to 350°F (180°C) and line a baking sheet with parchment paper.

Cut two of the beets into thin slices. Drizzle the remaining two beets with olive oil and a pinch of salt. Wrap them in foil and roast for 35 to 50 minutes, or until soft and fork tender. The time will depend on the size and freshness of your beets. Remove the beets from the oven, unwrap the foil, and set aside to cool. When they are cool to the touch, peel the skins. I like to hold them under running water and slide the skins off with my hands. Slice the beets and chill until ready to use.

In a large bowl, combine 2 tablespoons of the olive oil, the lemon juice, orange juice, white wine vinegar, Dijon mustard, and garlic. Add the raw beets and radishes to the bowl and season with a few generous pinches of salt and pepper. Toss, and let the raw vegetables marinate at room temperature for at least 20 minutes. Add the roasted beets, carrots, farro, and mint to the bowl and toss until well coated. Add the baby salad greens, chickpeas, if using, and feta cheese, if using, and toss again. Season to taste. Add a drizzle of olive oil and a squeeze of lemon, if desired.

VEGAN: Skip the cheese. | **GLUTEN-FREE:** Use quinoa. | *SERVES:* **4**

12

CORN

During my first day of second grade, the teacher went around the room and asked every child what they did over their summer break. My answer? "I ate corn." I'm not sure why that was the memory that summed up my summer. Maybe because I had just eaten it for dinner the night before . . . oh, and also every night in August. This wasn't grocery store corn—it's what we called "farm corn" (because it came from a local Illinois farm stand). Farm corn was definitely my first experience with the concept of eating seasonally, and it's how I learned it's always worth it to wait for the best possible version of any vegetable.

SEASON

SUMMER

This is an easy perfect summer salad. Serve it with whatever you're grilling!

CORN, TOMATO & MOZZARELLA SALAD

INGREDIENTS	*DIRECTIONS*
2 ears fresh corn, husked	Preheat a grill or grill pan to medium-high heat. Brush the corn with olive oil and grill, about 2 minutes per side, rotating until the kernels on all sides are tender and a few char marks form, about 10 minutes. Let cool, then slice the kernels off the cobs.
1 teaspoon (5 mL) extra-virgin olive oil, plus more for brushing	
2 cups (500 mL) chopped baby spinach	
½ cup (125 mL) halved cherry tomatoes	
1 cup (250 mL) small fresh mozzarella balls, sliced in half	Place the corn in a large bowl with the spinach, tomatoes, mozzarella, scallions, and basil. Toss with 1 teaspoon of olive oil, the sherry vinegar, and smoked paprika, if using. Season generously with salt and pepper.
¼ cup (60 mL) chopped scallions	
½ cup (125 mL) thinly sliced basil	
1 teaspoon (5 mL) sherry vinegar	
Sea salt and freshly ground black pepper	
¼ teaspoon (1 mL) smoked paprika (optional)	

VEGAN: Use diced avocado instead of mozzarella. | **GLUTEN-FREE** | *SERVES:* 4

GRILLED MEXICAN CORN SALAD

INGREDIENTS

4 ears fresh corn, husked

½ teaspoon (2 mL) extra-virgin olive oil

2 tablespoons (30 mL) adobo sauce from canned chipotles in adobo sauce

⅓ cup (75 mL) crumbled cotija or feta cheese

⅓ cup (75 mL) chopped cilantro, plus a few sprigs for garnish

Juice of ½ lime

Sea salt and freshly ground black pepper

DIRECTIONS

Preheat a grill or grill pan to medium-high heat. Brush the corn with the olive oil and grill, about 2 minutes per side, rotating it until the kernels on all sides are tender and a few char marks form, about 10 minutes.

Remove the corn from the heat and brush with the adobo sauce. Use a knife to slice the kernels off the cob. Toss with the crumbled cheese, cilantro, lime juice, and salt and pepper to taste. Add cilantro sprigs to garnish.

VEGAN: Use diced avocado instead of cheese. | **GLUTEN-FREE** | *SERVES:* **4** *AS A SIDE*

Growing up in the Midwest, the only way I knew to eat corn was with nothing but a pat of butter and a little salt. But here in Austin, corn comes *elote* style—with cheese and chipotle spices—and I can't get enough. Eat this as a salad or in tacos (page 123).

ELOTES & ROASTED CHICKPEA TACOS

INGREDIENTS

4 ears fresh corn, husked

1 teaspoon (5 mL) extra-virgin olive oil

2 tablespoons (30 mL) adobo sauce from canned chipotles in adobo sauce

⅓ cup (75 mL) crumbled cotija or feta cheese

⅓ cup (75 mL) chopped cilantro, plus a few sprigs for garnish

Juice of ½ lime

1 cup (250 mL) cooked chickpeas, drained and rinsed (page 285)

8 whole wheat flour tortillas, warmed or grilled

Lime wedges, for serving

Sea salt and freshly ground black pepper

Sriracha (optional)

DIRECTIONS

Preheat a grill or grill pan to medium-high heat. Brush the corn with ½ teaspoon of olive oil and grill, about 2 minutes per side, rotating it until the kernels on all sides are tender and a few char marks form, about 10 minutes.

Remove the corn from the heat and brush with the adobo sauce. Use a knife to slice the kernels off the cob. Toss with the crumbled cheese, cilantro, lime juice, and salt and pepper to taste.

In a small skillet, heat ½ teaspoon of olive oil over medium heat. Add the chickpeas, a pinch of salt, and pepper. Sauté until golden brown, about 5 minutes, shaking the pan to rotate them occasionally.

Fill each tortilla with the corn, chickpeas, and cilantro sprigs. Serve with lime wedges and sriracha, if desired, on the side.

VEGAN: Use diced avocado instead of cheese.

GLUTEN-FREE: Use corn tortillas.

SERVES: 4

SPICY CORNBREAD

INGREDIENTS

1 cup (250 mL) cornmeal

1 cup (250 mL) spelt flour or all-purpose flour

2 teaspoons (10 mL) baking powder

¼ teaspoon (1 mL) baking soda

1 teaspoon (5 mL) salt

¾ cup (175 mL) unsweetened almond milk, at room temperature

½ cup (125 mL) maple syrup

½ cup (125 mL) melted coconut oil, plus more for drizzling

1 teaspoon (5 mL) apple cider vinegar

½ cup (125 mL) corn kernels (fresh or frozen)

1 serrano pepper, sliced

DIRECTIONS

Preheat the oven to 350°F (180°C).

In a large bowl, stir together the cornmeal, flour, baking powder, baking soda, and salt. In a medium bowl, whisk together the almond milk, maple syrup, coconut oil, and apple cider vinegar.

Pour the wet ingredients into the bowl with the dry ingredients and stir until just combined. Fold in the corn kernels and sliced serrano pepper. Don't overmix.

Brush a 10-inch (25-cm) cast-iron skillet with a drizzle of coconut oil. Spread the batter into the skillet and bake for 20 to 22 minutes, or until a toothpick inserted comes out clean.

Cool for 15 minutes before serving.

VEGAN

SERVES: **8** TO **12**

This recipe can also be made in mini-skillet pans or muffin cups:
For eight 3½-inch (8.5-cm) mini-skillets—bake 18 to 20 minutes;
for a 12-cup muffin tin—bake 15 to 18 minutes.

GREEN TEA CUCUMBER SMOOTHIE

Add ½ small cucumber to a blender with ½ cup (125 mL)
coconut milk, 1 small apple, a frozen banana, and a handful of spinach.
Add 1 teaspoon (5 mL) matcha powder and blend until smooth.

13

CUCUMBER

TOSS THEM

into salads or noodle
bowls for crunch.

SLICE THEM

into thin rounds and make a
simple marinated cucumber salad
with a drizzle of rice vinegar,
sesame oil, and a pinch of sea salt.

BLEND THEM

into your green juice or
smoothie!

SEASON

SUMMER

GREEN GAZPACHO

1 large English cucumber, chopped (reserve ½ cup/125 mL for garnish)

6 small to medium yellow tomatoes, quartered, with juices

2 scallions

1 garlic clove

½ cup (125 mL) cilantro

¼ cup (60 mL) sherry vinegar

¼ cup (60 mL) extra-virgin olive oil, plus more for drizzling

½ cup (125 mL) raw sunflower seeds

Sea salt and freshly ground black pepper

½ serrano pepper (optional)

1 teaspoon (5 mL) honey or raw cane sugar (optional)

In a blender, combine the cucumber, tomatoes, scallions, garlic, cilantro, sherry vinegar, olive oil, sunflower seeds, and serrano pepper, if using. Blend until smooth and season to taste. Depending on the sweetness of your tomatoes, you may want to add a drizzle of honey or a few pinches of sugar. Chill for at least 30 minutes.

Garnish the soup with the reserved chopped cucumbers and a drizzle of olive oil.

VEGAN: Skip the honey. | **GLUTEN-FREE** | *SERVES:* **4**

I love soups all year round, but hot summer days call for this cool and refreshing gazpacho. If you can't find yellow tomatoes, use red ones— your soup won't be green, but it'll be delicious nonetheless.

CUCUMBER BASIL & WATERMELON SALAD

1 tablespoon (15 mL) tamari

1 small garlic clove, minced

½ teaspoon (2 mL) minced ginger

2 teaspoons (10 mL) fresh lime juice

2 teaspoons (10 mL) rice vinegar

3 cups (750 mL) ½-inch (1-cm) cubed watermelon, deseeded

1 English cucumber, chopped into ½-inch (1-cm) pieces (just over 2 cups/500 mL)

1 ripe mango, skin removed and chopped into ½-inch (1-cm) pieces

½ serrano pepper, thinly sliced

¼ cup (60 mL) chopped cilantro

¼ cup (60 mL) sliced basil

¼ cup (60 mL) salted peanuts, crushed and toasted (page 285)

DIRECTIONS

In a large bowl, whisk together the tamari, garlic, ginger, lime juice, and rice vinegar.

Add the watermelon, cucumber, mango, serrano pepper, cilantro, and basil. Chill for 30 minutes. Drain a little of the excess liquid before serving.

Serve with the crushed peanuts on top.

VEGAN | **GLUTEN-FREE**

SERVES: **4**

COLD SESAME
CUCUMBER NOODLES

INGREDIENTS

¼ cup (60 mL) rice vinegar

2 tablespoons (30 mL) tamari, plus more
to taste

1 tablespoon (15 mL) toasted sesame oil,
plus more for drizzling

1 tablespoon (15 mL) creamy peanut butter

2 garlic cloves, minced

2 teaspoons (10 mL) grated ginger

2 tablespoons (30 mL) chopped scallions

12 ounces (340 g) somen or soba noodles

1 large cucumber, julienned

2 tablespoons (30 mL) sesame seeds

OPTIONAL ADD-INS

Snap peas, blanched for 1 minute

Tofu cubes

Edamame

Sliced radishes

Diced avocado

DIRECTIONS

In a large bowl, whisk together the rice
vinegar, tamari, sesame oil, peanut butter,
garlic, and ginger. Stir in the scallions.

Bring a large pot of salted water to a boil.
Prepare the noodles according to the
instructions on the package, cooking until
al dente. Drain, then chill the noodles in a
bowl of ice water for about 1 minute. Drain,
then add the noodles to the large bowl.

Add the cucumber and toss to combine.
Add the snap peas, tofu, and additional
vegetables, if using.

Season with more tamari, to taste. Finish
with a drizzle of sesame oil and sprinkle with
the sesame seeds. Chill until ready to serve.

VEGAN | **GLUTEN-FREE:** Use 100% buckwheat soba noodles or brown rice pasta. | *SERVES:* **4**

14

EGGPLANT

Don't be intimidated by eggplant, it's so versatile! Bake it, grill it, or use it to make delicious veggie meatballs (page 141). I also love to broil small eggplant with a miso glaze. Here is a version of Nasu Dengaku, one of my favorite dishes from our travels to Japan.

✕✕✕✕✕✕✕✕✕✕✕ MISO-GLAZED JAPANESE EGGPLANT: ✕✕✕✕✕✕✕✕✕✕✕

In a small saucepan over medium heat, combine ¼ cup (60 mL) white miso paste, ¼ cup (60 mL) mirin (or rice vinegar), and ¼ cup (60 mL) cane sugar. Whisk continuously until the sugar dissolves. Slice eggplants in half, place them on a baking sheet, and generously brush them with the glaze. Broil until the eggplant is tender and the glaze is dark brown and bubbling.

SEASON

SUMMER

1 Slice the eggplant and make your breading.

2 Bread the eggplant and place in a dish layered with tomato sauce.

3 Grate fresh pecorino cheese on top.

4 Bake until the eggplant is tender and the outside is crispy.

CRISPY BAKED EGGPLANT

1 large eggplant, sliced ¼ inch (0.5 cm) thick (12 to 17 slices)

½ cup (125 mL) almond milk

2 teaspoons (10 mL) cornstarch

Extra-virgin olive oil, for drizzling

1 can (14.5 ounces/411 g) diced tomatoes

Balsamic vinegar, for drizzling

½ cup (125 mL) grated pecorino cheese

Pinch of red pepper flakes

Sea salt and freshly ground black pepper

BREADING

¾ cup (175 mL) hemp seeds

3 tablespoons (45 mL) nutritional yeast

3 tablespoons (45 mL) sunflower seeds

1 garlic clove

¾ cup (175 mL) panko bread crumbs

1 teaspoon (5 mL) oregano

½ teaspoon (2 mL) red pepper flakes

Sea salt and freshly ground black pepper

Preheat the oven to 400°F (200°C).

Pat dry the eggplant and lay on paper towels. Sprinkle with salt and let sit while you prep everything else. Pat dry occasionally.

Make the breading: In a food processor, pulse the hemp seeds, nutritional yeast, sunflower seeds, garlic, panko, oregano, red pepper flakes, and pinches of salt and pepper. Transfer to a shallow bowl.

In another shallow bowl, whisk together the almond milk and cornstarch.

Drizzle a 9 x 13-inch (23 x 33-cm) pan with olive oil. Add the tomatoes, drizzle with balsamic vinegar, and add pinches of salt and pepper. Spread to evenly coat the bottom of the pan.

Dip each eggplant slice in the almond milk, shake off any excess liquid, then dip in the breading mixture. Place in the pan on top of the tomatoes, allowing the eggplant slices to overlap slightly. Top with the pecorino cheese, a drizzle of olive oil, and the red pepper flakes. Bake, covered, for 15 minutes. Uncover and bake an additional 15 to 18 minutes, or until the eggplant is tender and the top is crispy.

VEGAN: Skip the cheese.

SERVES: 4

GRILLED EGGPLANT & SUMMER VEGGIE PASTA

1 large eggplant

2 medium zucchini

1 red bell pepper, stem and ribs removed

8 large cremini mushrooms

Extra-virgin olive oil, for drizzling

8 ounces (225 g) shell pasta or similar small shaped pasta

½ cup (125 mL) quick pickled onions (page 187)

½ cup (125 mL) basil leaves, torn

Pinch of red pepper flakes

Sherry vinegar, for drizzling

Pinches of dried oregano

Pinches of smoked paprika

Sea salt and freshly ground black pepper

Freshly grated Parmesan cheese (optional)

Heat a grill or grill pan to high heat.

Slice the eggplant vertically into 1-inch (2.5-cm)-thick planks. Slice the zucchini in half lengthwise. Slice the bell pepper vertically into 4 pieces. Drizzle the eggplant, zucchini, bell pepper, and whole mushrooms with olive oil and pinches of salt and pepper. Grill until all the vegetables are charred on both sides, 5 to 8 minutes per side.

Meanwhile, bring a large pot of salted water to a boil. Prepare the pasta according to the instructions on the package, cooking until al dente. Drain and place in a bowl.

Chop the eggplant, zucchini, and bell pepper into 1-inch (2.5-cm) pieces and slice the cremini mushrooms into quarters. Toss the vegetables with the pasta along with the pickled onions, basil, a pinch of pepper, and the red pepper flakes. Drizzle with the sherry vinegar and oregano and smoked paprika. Toss and season to taste. Serve with freshly grated Parmesan cheese if you like.

VEGAN: Skip the cheese. | **GLUTEN-FREE:** Use brown rice pasta. | *SERVES:* **4**

EGGPLANT & MUSHROOM "MEATBALLS"

INGREDIENTS

Extra-virgin olive oil, for drizzling

1 medium yellow onion, finely chopped

8 ounces (225 g) cremini mushrooms, de-stemmed and chopped

1 small eggplant, chopped (about 8 ounces/225 g)

1 teaspoon (5 mL) balsamic vinegar

2 teaspoons (10 mL) tamari

½ cup (125 mL) walnuts

1 cup (250 mL) cooked millet (page 284)

1 cup (250 mL) panko bread crumbs

12 ounces (340 g) brown rice spaghetti

1 recipe simple fresh tomato sauce (page 251) or your favorite marinara sauce

Sea salt and freshly ground black pepper

DIRECTIONS

Preheat the oven to 400°F (200°C). Line a large baking sheet with parchment paper.

In a large skillet, heat a drizzle of olive oil over medium heat. Add the onion and cook until soft, about 2 minutes. Add the mushrooms and a pinch of salt and pepper, and cook until browned and soft, 5 to 8 minutes. Add the eggplant and another pinch of salt and pepper and cook another 5 minutes. Add the balsamic vinegar and tamari and cook 2 minutes, or until everything is well browned and soft. Taste and adjust the seasonings. Remove the mixture from the heat and let cool slightly.

In a food processor, pulse the walnuts. Add the mushroom/eggplant mixture and pulse two to three times until just combined. Transfer the mixture to a large bowl and add the cooked millet. Mix well. Form the mixture into sixteen 1½-inch (4-cm) balls and roll in the panko. Place the eggplant balls on the baking sheet and refrigerate for 20 minutes. Drizzle with olive oil and bake for 35 to 40 minutes, rotating halfway through.

Bring a large pot of salted water to a boil. Prepare the spaghetti according to the instructions on the package, cooking until al dente. Drain the pasta.

Serve the spaghetti and "meatballs" with the simple fresh tomato sauce.

NOTE "Meatballs" can be made ahead and refrigerated for several hours or overnight.

VEGAN

SERVES: 4

COLLARD GREENS:
nature's burrito wrapper.
Blanch them slightly to
take off the raw bite,
stuff them with your
favorite filling,
wrap, and eat.

CURLY KALE:
This is great for kale
salads (page 157).

ARUGULA:
my favorite
green to use
in a salad.
Nothing
beats its
peppery bite
(pages 155
and 255).

15

GREENS

LACINATO KALE (OR DINOSAUR KALE):

Chop it and add it at the end of soups and
pastas so it wilts but stays vibrant.

SEASON

VARIES

OTHER GORGEOUS GREENS, NOT PICTURED: chard, bok choy, mustard greens, amaranth greens . . . the list goes on and on.

SWISS CHARD & WHITE BEAN TACOS

INGREDIENTS

5 Swiss chard leaves

1 teaspoon (5 mL) extra-virgin olive oil

1 medium yellow onion, sliced

2 garlic cloves, minced

¼ teaspoon (1 mL) dried oregano

½ cup (125 mL) cooked cannellini beans, drained and rinsed (page 285)

8 tortillas

⅓ cup (75 mL) crumbled feta cheese

Handful of cilantro leaves

Creamy tomatillo salsa (page 281)

Sea salt and freshly ground black pepper

DIRECTIONS

Roll the Swiss chard leaves lengthwise, including ribs and stems, and slice into thin strips. Chop the thicker parts of the chard stems.

In a large skillet, heat the olive oil over medium heat. Add the sliced onion and a few pinches of salt. Sauté the onion until soft and golden brown around the edges, about 7 minutes. Add the chard stems and stir and cook for about a minute. Add the garlic, chard leaves, and a pinch of salt and pepper. Gently toss until the chard wilts down, about 30 seconds. Add the oregano and the cannellini beans. Toss to combine and then remove from the heat.

Fill the tortillas with the chard filling and top each with some feta cheese. Serve with cilantro and the creamy tomatillo salsa.

VEGAN: Skip the cheese.   **GLUTEN-FREE:** Use corn tortillas.   *SERVES:* 4

Toss any
vegetable with
this easy peanut
noodle recipe.
It's so delicious
and versatile.
Make a big
batch and pack
it up for lunch
all week.

PEANUT NOODLE KALE BOWLS

INGREDIENTS

SAUCE

3 tablespoons (45 mL) creamy peanut butter

1 tablespoon (15 mL) toasted sesame oil

1½ teaspoons (7 mL) tamari,
plus more for serving

1 teaspoon (5 mL) freshly grated ginger

1 garlic clove, minced

1 teaspoon (5 mL) sriracha

3 tablespoons (45 mL) water

- -

6 ounces (170 g) soba noodles

6 cups (1.5 L) loosely packed chopped kale

3 sliced watermelon radishes or 6 sliced
small red radishes

½ cup (125 mL) frozen edamame, thawed

2 tablespoons (30 mL) sesame seeds

DIRECTIONS

Make the sauce: In a small bowl, whisk together the peanut butter, sesame oil, tamari, ginger, garlic, sriracha, and water.

Bring a large pot of salted water to a boil. Prepare the noodles according to the package directions, cooking until al dente. When the noodles are cooked, transfer them to a large bowl, keeping your soba cooking water on the stove. Using the same water, blanch the kale for 30 seconds, or until wilted but still bright green. Drain, and add the kale to the bowl with the soba noodles.

Add the sauce to the noodles and kale and toss to incorporate. Garnish with the sliced radishes and edamame and sprinkle with the sesame seeds. Serve with additional tamari.

VEGAN | **GLUTEN-FREE:** Use 100% buckwheat soba noodles or brown rice pasta. | *SERVES:* **4**

I could probably write a book *just* about soups. They're comforting to make and comforting to eat, and I can pack in tons of vegetables. Soup is love, and I really love this one.

KALE & FENNEL VEGETABLE SOUP

INGREDIENTS

2 tablespoons (30 mL) extra-virgin olive oil

1 small yellow onion, chopped

1 medium fennel bulb, sliced

2 garlic cloves, minced

2 medium carrots, chopped

3 sprigs fresh thyme

1 cup (250 mL) chopped savoy cabbage

⅓ cup (75 mL) dry white wine

4 cups (1 L) vegetable broth

1-inch (2.5-cm) piece of Parmesan cheese rind

1 cup (250 mL) cooked cannellini beans, drained and rinsed (page 285)

2 cups (500 mL) chopped kale

1½ tablespoons (22 mL) fresh lemon juice

½ cup (125 mL) chopped fennel fronds

Sea salt and freshly ground black pepper

DIRECTIONS

In a large pot, heat the olive oil over medium heat. Add the onion and a few pinches of salt and pepper and cook until the onion is translucent, about 8 minutes. Add the fennel, garlic, carrots, and thyme. Cook until the carrots begin to soften, 8 to 10 minutes, stirring occasionally. Add the cabbage and another pinch of salt and pepper and cook until the cabbage is soft, about 5 more minutes.

Add the white wine, stir, and let the wine cook off, about 1 minute.

Add the vegetable broth, Parmesan cheese rind, and cannellini beans. Reduce the heat and let the soup simmer until the vegetables are tender, about 15 minutes. Add the kale and simmer for 5 more minutes. Add the lemon juice, then taste and adjust the seasonings. Discard the Parmesan cheese rind and garnish with fennel fronds.

VEGAN: Skip the Parmesan cheese. | **GLUTEN-FREE** | *SERVES:* **4**

MANGO AVOCADO COLLARD WRAPS

INGREDIENTS

2 cups (500 mL) cooked brown rice (page 284)

¼ cup (60 mL) sesame seeds

8 medium collard leaves

1 red bell pepper, stem and ribs removed, sliced into thin strips

1 mango, peeled and sliced into thin strips

1 small cucumber, sliced into thin strips

1 avocado, pitted and sliced

1 recipe carrot-ginger sauce (page 287)

Tamari, for dipping

½ cup (125 mL) microgreens (optional)

DIRECTIONS

Mix the cooked brown rice with the sesame seeds and set aside.

Prepare a large pot of boiling water and a large bowl of ice water. Drop the collard greens one at a time into the boiling water and blanch for 30 seconds. Remove and immediately immerse in ice water to stop the cooking process. Keep the greens in the ice water long enough to cool completely, about 15 seconds. Place on paper towels to dry.

Slice off the coarse part of the collard stem. Assemble each leaf with brown rice, bell pepper, mango, cucumber, and avocado. Top with microgreens, if using. Roll like a taco or a little burrito and serve with the carrot-ginger sauce and tamari for dipping.

TIP Easily change up these ingredients to make entirely different wraps. Add black beans and swap the carrot-ginger sauce for salsa and you have a Tex-Mex version!

VEGAN | GLUTEN-FREE

SERVES: **4**

MISO-BRAISED MUSTARD GREENS

1 teaspoon (5 mL) white miso paste

¼ cup (60 mL) warm water

Several bunches of Asian mustard greens or baby bok choy, about 20 leaves

1 teaspoon (5 mL) extra-virgin olive oil

½ teaspoon (2 mL) rice vinegar

½ teaspoon (2 mL) maple syrup or honey

Toasted sesame oil, for drizzling

Sesame seeds, for sprinkling

In a small bowl, whisk together the miso paste and water.

Trim off the rough bottoms of the mustard greens, separate the leaves, and rinse under running water. Pat dry.

In a large skillet, heat the olive oil over medium heat. Add the mustard greens and cook about 2 minutes, turning occasionally. Add half the miso water, cover, and let cook until the stems start to soften, about 2 more minutes. If the skillet is getting dry, add more miso water.

Add the rice vinegar and maple syrup and toss. Transfer to a serving plate, drizzle with sesame oil, and sprinkle with sesame seeds.

VEGAN: Skip the honey. | **GLUTEN-FREE** | *SERVES:* **4** *AS A SIDE*

WATERCRESS, FETA & FARRO SALAD

DRESSING

2 tablespoons (30 mL) extra-virgin olive oil

2 tablespoons (30 mL) apple cider vinegar

1 garlic clove, minced

¼ teaspoon (1 mL) maple syrup

Sea salt and freshly ground black pepper

- -

2 cups (500 mL) cooked farro (page 284)

1 small watermelon radish, thinly sliced and chopped

⅓ cup (75 mL) dried tart cherries or cranberries

¼ cup (60 mL) crushed walnuts

⅓ cup (75 mL) crumbled feta cheese

2 cups (500 mL) watercress or arugula

1 cup (250 mL) basil leaves, torn

½ cup (125 mL) mint leaves

Sea salt and freshly ground black pepper

Make the dressing: In a small bowl, whisk together the olive oil, apple cider vinegar, garlic, maple syrup, and pinches of salt and pepper.

Toss the cooked farro with the radish slices, tart cherries, walnuts, feta cheese, and dressing. Add the watercress, basil, and mint and gently toss again. Season with salt and pepper to taste.

SERVES: **4**

1 | Wash and dry the kale.

2 | Remove the stems and tear the leaves into small pieces.

3 | Drizzle with olive oil, a squeeze of lemon juice, and a pinch of sea salt.

4 | Massage the leaves until they are soft and tender.

HOW TO MAKE A KALE SALAD

After you massage the kale leaves, build your salad.
These are a few of my favorite combinations:

chili-roasted sweet potato cubes	thinly sliced fennel	carrot ribbons	roasted winter squash
+	+	+	+
diced avocado	roasted chickpeas with garlic	sliced cucumbers	dried cranberries
+	+	+	+
black beans	Dijon mustard	basil or mint	chopped almonds
+	+	+	+
feta cheese	pine nuts	scoop of hummus	apple cider vinegar
+	+	+	+
toasted pepitas	shaved Parmesan cheese	hemp seeds	feta or goat cheese

TIP:

*I find that kale bunches vary in texture and taste.
If yours is still a little tough and bitter after massaging it,
add something sweet for balance: a squeeze of fresh orange juice,
a drizzle of honey, or a drizzle of maple syrup.*

TIP:

Heartier herbs like
rosemary and sage
freeze well.

PALLARES
SOLSONA

Pictured:
flat-leaf parsley,
cilantro, basil,
thyme, purple
sage, tarragon,
oregano, mint

16

HERBS

Herbs are the easiest way to punch up flavor in your food (after lemons, of course). They can be expensive to buy in little packages, so I recommend trying to grow a few yourself. I'm no green thumb, but I've had decent luck with basil, mint, thyme, oregano, and sage. When I cook with herbs, I always add the lighter herbs (basil, mint, chives) at the very end so they stay bright and vibrant.

SEASON

SPRING / SUMMER

CASHEW & CAPER DILL SPREAD

INGREDIENTS

1 cup (250 mL) raw unsalted cashews, soaked 3 to 4 hours, preferably overnight

½ cup (125 mL) fresh water

Juice of ½ small lemon

½ teaspoon (2 mL) lemon zest

1 garlic clove, peeled

2 tablespoons (30 mL) extra-virgin olive oil

2 teaspoons (10 mL) capers

½ cup (125 mL) fresh dill, coarsely chopped; reserve a few for garnish

Baguette or crackers, for serving

Sea salt and freshly ground black pepper

1 recipe quick pickled onions (page 187), for serving (optional)

DIRECTIONS

Drain and rinse the cashews and place them in a high-speed blender. Add the water, lemon juice, lemon zest, garlic, and olive oil. Puree until smooth. Add the capers and the dill. Season with salt and pepper and blend until well combined. Taste and adjust the seasonings. Chill until ready to serve.

Slather onto warm baguette slices and garnish with fresh dill and quick pickled onions, if desired.

Yield: 1½ cups (375 mL)

TIP Allergic to nuts? Sub in sunflower seeds. No dill? Use soft herbs like basil, mint, or tarragon instead.

VEGAN | **GLUTEN-FREE:** Use gluten-free bread or crackers.

SPRING LEEK SOUP
WITH PURPLE SAGE

4 medium leeks

2 teaspoons (10 mL) extra-virgin olive oil

2 Yukon Gold potatoes, chopped into
½-inch (1-cm) cubes

4 garlic cloves, minced

¼ cup (60 mL) loosely packed sage,
coarsely chopped

¼ cup (60 mL) dry white wine

4 cups (1 L) vegetable broth

¼ cup (60 mL) loosely packed thyme
sprigs, coarsely chopped

1½ cups (375 mL) cooked cannellini beans,
drained and rinsed (page 285)

1 to 2 tablespoons (15 to 30 mL) fresh
lemon juice

1 recipe traditional pesto (page 275)

Crusty bread

Sea salt and freshly ground black pepper

Slice the white and light green parts of the leek into rings. Using a strainer, rinse the leeks thoroughly.

Heat the olive oil in a large pot over medium heat. Add the leeks and a pinch of salt and pepper. Stir and cook until the leeks begin to soften, about 2 minutes. Add the potatoes and another few generous pinches of salt, and cook until the potatoes begin to soften, about 2 minutes.

Add the garlic and sage and continue cooking for 1 more minute. Stir in the white wine and cook for 1 minute. Add the vegetable broth and thyme. Reduce the heat to a simmer and cook until the potatoes are tender, about 18 minutes, adding the cannellini beans during the last 5 minutes of cooking time.

Add the lemon juice, then taste and adjust the seasonings, adding more salt and pepper as desired.

Serve with traditional pesto and crusty bread on the side.

VEGAN: Omit the cheese from the pesto recipe. | **GLUTEN-FREE** | *SERVES:* **4**

AVOCADO PESTO
MOZZARELLA TARTINES

INGREDIENTS

8 slices whole-grain bread

Extra-virgin olive oil, for drizzling

16 fresh sage leaves, de-stemmed

1 (8-ounce/225-g) ball fresh mozzarella, sliced

1 avocado, sliced

Few leaves of watercress

Few sprigs of fresh thyme

1 recipe any pesto (page 275)

Sea salt and freshly ground black pepper

DIRECTIONS

Drizzle the bread with olive oil, then toast in a toaster or on a grill.

In a small skillet over medium heat, drizzle enough olive oil to coat the bottom of the pan. When the oil shimmers, add the sage leaves and lightly fry until they turn vibrant green without browning, 10 to 15 seconds on each side. Transfer to a paper towel to drain any excess oil.

Top each piece of toasted bread with slices of mozzarella, avocado, watercress, thyme, sage, and dollops of pesto. Season with salt and pepper. Serve with the extra pesto on the side.

VEGAN: Skip the cheese.   **GLUTEN-FREE:** Use gluten-free bread.   *SERVES:* **4**

I love the peppery bite of watercress, but skip it if you don't have any, or use a few arugula leaves instead.

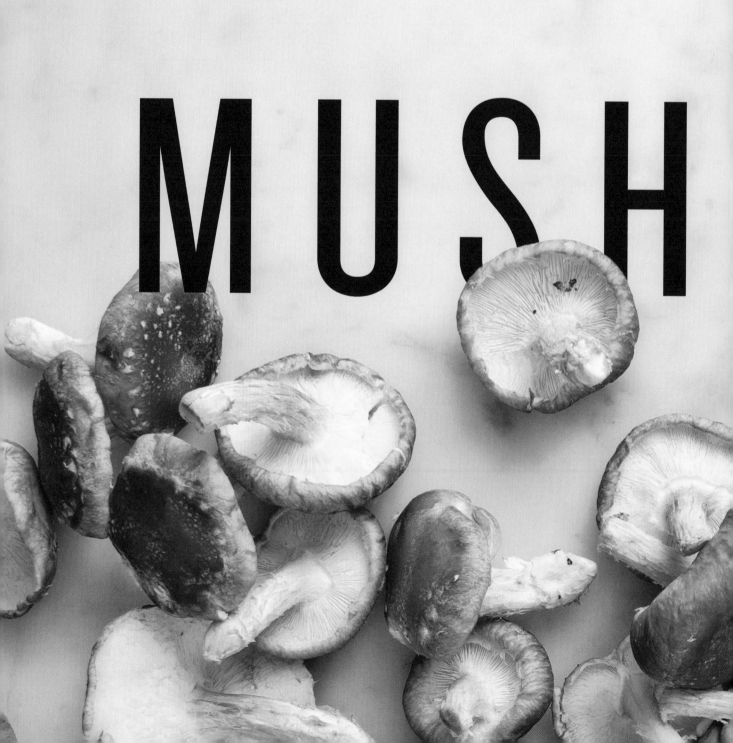

MUSH

17
ROOMS

Unlike most people I know, I never really loved or hated mushrooms. I remember picking raw ones out of salads only because they seemed sort of plain. That is, until I met Jack. My husband, Jack, is the biggest mushroom lover of them all. At restaurants, he would order portobello sandwiches, mushroom risotto, and funghi pizzas (while making corny jokes about being a "fun guy"). Suffice it to say, I fell in love with both him and mushrooms at the same time.

SEASON

VARIES

PORTOBELLO SLIDERS WITH PEPITA PESTO

8 small portobello mushrooms

Extra-virgin olive oil, for drizzling

Balsamic vinegar, for drizzling

Tamari, for drizzling

8 slider buns, toasted

1 tomato, sliced

½ cup (125 mL) microgreens

1 recipe pepita pesto (page 275)

Freshly ground black pepper

Heat a grill or grill pan to medium heat.

Prepare the mushrooms by removing the stems and cleaning the caps with a damp cloth or paper towel. Place the mushrooms in a medium bowl and drizzle with olive oil, balsamic vinegar, tamari, and pepper. Toss until well coated. (I use my hands to rub it all over until they are fully coated on both sides.)

Place the mushrooms, gill side down, on the grill or grill pan. Cook about 10 minutes per side, or until the mushrooms are tender.

Place the mushrooms on the toasted buns and top each with a tomato slice, microgreens, and a generous slather of pepita pesto.

VEGAN

SERVES: **4**

CRISPY SHIITAKE BLT

8 ounces (225 g) shiitake mushrooms

2 tablespoons (30 mL) extra-virgin olive oil

1 tablespoon (15 mL) tamari

4 slices whole-grain bread

2 teaspoons (10 mL) mayonnaise

Small handful of arugula

2 small tomatoes, sliced

Preheat the oven to 300°F (150°C). Line a large baking sheet with parchment paper.

Prepare the mushrooms by removing the stems and cleaning with a damp cloth or paper towel. Then slice the mushrooms.

Toss the sliced mushrooms with the olive oil and tamari until well coated and place on the baking sheet so that the mushrooms are not touching one another. Bake for 30 to 40 minutes, tossing halfway through, until the mushrooms are shriveled up and crispy.

Assemble the sandwiches on the bread with a slather of mayo, the arugula, sliced tomatoes, and the crispy shiitake mushrooms.

VEGAN: Use vegan mayonnaise.

SERVES: **2**

SOBA WITH MUSHROOMS & CRUMBLED HAZELNUTS

1 small leek

8 cups (2 L) mixed mushrooms (creminis, shiitakes), sliced

1 tablespoon (15 mL) salted butter

2 garlic cloves, minced

8 ounces (225 g) soba noodles

1 tablespoon (15 mL) rice vinegar

1 teaspoon (5 mL) tamari

½ cup (125 mL) roasted hazelnuts (page 285), pulsed in food processor into fine crumbs

1 cup (250 mL) microgreens

Sea salt and freshly ground black pepper

Slice the white and light green parts of the leek into rings. Using a strainer, rinse the leeks thoroughly. Prepare the mushrooms by removing the stems and then cleaning with a damp cloth or paper towel.

In a large skillet, heat the butter over medium heat. Add the leek, mushrooms, and garlic and season with salt and pepper. Cook until browned, about 8 minutes, stirring only occasionally.

Meanwhile, bring a large pot of water to a boil. Cook the soba noodles according to the package directions. Drain and rinse.

To the mushroom mixture, stir in the rice vinegar, tamari, and crushed hazelnuts. Remove from the heat and toss with the soba noodles. Season to taste.

Transfer to plates, top with microgreens, and serve.

VEGAN: Use olive oil instead of butter.

GLUTEN-FREE: Use 100% buckwheat soba or brown rice noodles.

SERVES: **4**

SHIITAKE & SPINACH MISO SOUP

3 cups (750 mL) shiitake mushrooms

1 tablespoon (15 mL) extra-virgin olive oil

⅓ cup (75 mL) scallions, finely chopped

2 garlic cloves, minced

2 teaspoons (10 mL) grated ginger

5 cups (1.25 L) water

3 tablespoons (45 mL) white miso paste

4 ounces (115 g) soba noodles or somen or capellini pasta

2 cups (500 mL) packed baby spinach

1 tablespoon (15 mL) tamari, plus more to taste

½ teaspoon (2 mL) toasted sesame oil, plus more for drizzling

1 tablespoon (15 mL) rice vinegar

¼ teaspoon (1 mL) red pepper flakes

Sea salt

Prepare the mushrooms by removing the stems and cleaning with a damp cloth or paper towel. Then slice the mushrooms.

Heat the olive oil in a large saucepan over medium heat. Add the mushrooms and a few pinches of salt and stir. Let the mushrooms cook until soft, about 5 minutes, stirring only occasionally. Add the scallions, garlic, and ginger and cook 1 more minute. Add the water and bring to a low simmer. Scoop some of the simmering water into a small bowl and add the miso paste, stirring until it dissolves, then add it back into the soup pot. Simmer over low heat for 15 minutes.

Bring a medium pot of water to a boil. Prepare the noodles according to the instructions on the package. Drain the noodles and add them to the soup pot, followed by the spinach, tamari, sesame oil, rice vinegar, and red pepper flakes. Stir until the spinach is wilted. Season to taste with tamari and a drizzle of toasted sesame oil.

NOTE   Add a poached egg or tofu cubes to make a meal.

VEGAN | **GLUTEN-FREE:** Use 100% buckwheat soba or brown rice noodles. | *SERVES:* **4** *AS A SIDE OR STARTER*

18

Onions

There is an onion in nearly every recipe in this book.
They're an essential staple for building flavor. But the alliums that really
get me all choked up are the leeks and spring onions you find at the
farmers market in the spring. They're so sweet and tender. Grill them
simply (page 179) and serve with mint pesto. If there are any left over, chop
them and fold them into your scrambled eggs the next morning.

SEASON

VARIES

GRILLED LEEKS
WITH MINT PESTO

|

MINT PESTO

½ cup (125 mL) pistachios

1 garlic clove

2 tablespoons (30 mL) fresh lemon juice

1 cup (250 mL) peas (blanched 1 minute if fresh; thawed if frozen)

1 cup (250 mL) loosely packed fresh mint

¼ cup (60 mL) extra-virgin olive oil

Sea salt and freshly ground black pepper

- -

8 medium to large leeks

Extra-virgin olive oil, for drizzling

Sea salt and freshly ground black pepper

Make the mint pesto: In a small food processor, combine the pistachios, garlic, and a few pinches of salt and pepper. Pulse until combined. Add the lemon juice, peas, and mint and pulse again. With the blade running, drizzle in the olive oil and puree until smooth. Taste and adjust the seasonings.

Trim and discard the tough dark green ends from the leeks. Trim the root hairs, leaving the base of the root intact so the leeks don't fall apart on the grill. Slice each leek in half lengthwise and rinse thoroughly to remove dirt and sand.

Prepare a large pot of salted boiling water and a large bowl of ice water. Drop the leeks into the boiling water and blanch for 2 minutes. Remove and immediately immerse in the ice water to stop the cooking process. Keep in the ice water long enough to cool completely, about 15 seconds. Drain and place on paper towels to dry.

Heat a grill or grill pan to medium-high heat. Drizzle the leeks with olive oil and pinches of salt and pepper. Grill until charred on both sides, about 5 minutes per side. Remove from the grill and brush with the mint pesto.

TIP   Use only the freshest peak-season leeks for this one.

VEGAN | **GLUTEN-FREE**   *SERVES:* **4**

SPRING ONION PIZZAS

1 recipe homemade pizza dough (page 285)

Cornmeal, for sprinkling

6 to 10 thin spring onions or scallions, sliced into vertical strips

Balsamic vinegar, for drizzling

1 tablespoon (15 mL) extra-virgin olive oil

½ garlic clove, minced

1 (8-ounce/225-g) ball fresh mozzarella cheese, sliced

1 cup (250 mL) finely chopped herbs (a mix of basil, parsley, and tarragon)

Pinches of red pepper flakes

Prepare the homemade pizza dough.

Preheat the oven to 450°F (230°C).

On a lightly floured flat surface, divide the dough into 2 balls and roll each into a 10-inch (25-cm) oval shape. Add flour as needed to prevent sticking. Place the pizzas on a baking sheet sprinkled with cornmeal.

On a plate, toss the spring onions with a drizzle of balsamic vinegar. In a small bowl, mix the olive oil with the minced garlic and brush onto the dough. Top the pizza dough with the mozzarella slices and spring onion strips.

Bake for 10 to 12 minutes, or until the onions are soft and the pizza crust is golden brown.

Top the pizzas with the chopped herbs and a few pinches of red pepper flakes.

SERVES: 4

QUINOA TACOS WITH QUICK PICKLED ONIONS

1 tablespoon (15 mL) extra-virgin olive oil

1 cup (250 mL) diced yellow onion

2 garlic cloves, minced

½ teaspoon (2 mL) ground cumin

½ teaspoon (2 mL) ground coriander

2 cups (500 mL) cooked quinoa (page 284)

1½ cups (375 mL) cooked black beans, drained and rinsed (page 285)

⅓ cup (75 mL) crumbled feta cheese

Juice of 1 lime

8 tortillas

½ cup (125 mL) quick pickled onions (page 187)

1 avocado, diced

½ cup (125 mL) loosely packed cilantro

Sea salt and freshly ground black pepper

1 recipe mango-basil salsa (page 281) (optional)

In a medium skillet, heat the olive oil over medium-low heat. Add the onion and pinches of salt and pepper. Cook until soft and lightly browned, 5 to 6 minutes. Add the garlic, cumin, and coriander and stir.

Add the quinoa and black beans and cook until warmed through, 2 more minutes. Remove from the heat and stir in the feta cheese and lime juice. Season with salt and pepper to taste.

Fill each tortilla with the quinoa/black bean mixture. Serve with the pickled onions, avocado, cilantro, and mango-basil salsa, if using.

VEGAN: Skip the cheese. | **GLUTEN-FREE:** Use corn tortillas. | *SERVES:* **4**

SPRING LEEK & LEMON PASTA

2 medium leeks

8 ounces (227 g) whole-grain pasta

1 tablespoon (15 mL) extra-virgin olive oil

5 radishes, sliced in half

½ cup (125 mL) cooked chickpeas, drained and rinsed (page 285)

1 garlic clove, minced

3 cups (750 mL) baby kale or amaranth

Juice and zest of ½ lemon

1 recipe mint pesto (page 275)

½ cup (125 mL) basil, finely chopped

¼ teaspoon (1 mL) red pepper flakes

Sea salt and freshly ground black pepper

Slice the white and light green parts of the leek into rings. Using a strainer, rinse the leeks thoroughly.

Bring a large pot of salted water to a boil. Prepare the pasta according to the instructions on the package, cooking until al dente. Drain the pasta, reserving ½ cup (125 mL) of the pasta water.

In a medium skillet, heat the olive oil over medium heat. Add the leeks and a pinch of salt and pepper and stir. Cook for 3 minutes or until the leeks start to soften. Add the radishes, cut side down, along with the chickpeas, and let them cook for 2 minutes. Turn and cook for 2 more minutes.

Stir in the garlic, greens, and lemon juice. Once the greens are lightly wilted, stir in the pasta and ½ cup (125 mL) of the pesto. Stir in the reserved pasta water, a few tablespoons at a time, as needed to loosen the pasta. Taste and season with salt and black pepper.

Remove from the heat and transfer to a platter or bowl. Top with the basil, lemon zest, and red pepper flakes.

VEGAN | **GLUTEN-FREE:** Use brown rice pasta.

SERVES: **4**

1 Thinly slice a red onion.

2 Place the onion slices in a jar with a tight lid.

3 Add the vinegar, sugar, salt, and water and shake gently.

4 Chill in the fridge for at least 1 hour.

QUICK PICKLED ONIONS

1 medium red onion (6 ounces/170 g)

½ cup (125 mL) white wine vinegar

Pinch of cane sugar

Pinch of sea salt

¼ cup (60 mL) warm water

Cut the onion in half and use a mandoline, if you have one, to cut each half into thin slices. Place the sliced onion in a tight-lidded jar just large enough to hold all of the onion.

Add the white wine vinegar, cane sugar, and salt and shake gently. Add warm water so that it covers the onion and shake again. Gently pack the onion down into the jar and chill for at least 1 hour. Store in the fridge for up to 2 weeks.

VEGAN | **GLUTEN-FREE**

Add to salads, tacos, sandwiches, wraps . . . Everyday meals can be elevated by a tangy pop of pickled onions.

19

P E A S

My husband, Jack, will eat any type of food under the sun with the exception of three things: beets, grapefruit, and peas. Every time I so much as mention these things, all I hear about is Miss Theresa and the mushy peas she forced him to eat in preschool. To be honest, I love the challenge of sneaking these foods in—at first I blended peas into pesto and he didn't even notice. After my secret was out, I realized I could put them in anything as long as it just tasted good.

SEASON

SPRING

SPRING PEA & MINT CROSTINI

6 to 8 slices whole-grain bread

Extra-virgin olive oil, for drizzling

¾ cup (175 mL) ricotta cheese

½ cup (125 mL) peas (blanched 1 minute if fresh; thawed if frozen)

2 radishes, thinly sliced

¼ cup (60 mL) crumbled feta cheese

Small bunch of mint leaves

Sea salt and freshly ground black pepper

Toast or grill the bread with a drizzle of olive oil. Top each slice with a slather of ricotta cheese, a few peas, the radish slices, crumbled feta cheese, and mint leaves. Season with salt and pepper to taste.

VEGAN: Use sun "cheese" (page 286) instead of ricotta and skip the feta cheese.

SERVES: **4**

FETA & PEA TENDRIL OMELETTE

4 large eggs

Extra-virgin olive oil, for drizzling

⅓ cup (75 mL) pea tendrils, lightly torn

2 tablespoons (30 mL) crumbled feta cheese

2 tablespoons (30 mL) cooked peas (blanched 1 minute if fresh; thawed if frozen)

½ avocado, diced

Pinch of red pepper flakes

Sea salt and freshly ground black pepper

In a medium bowl, whisk the eggs together with a pinch of salt.

In a small skillet, heat a drizzle of olive oil over medium heat. Pour half of the eggs into the skillet and use a rubber spatula to gently push the cooked portion of the eggs toward the center. Lift and tilt the pan gently to swirl the eggs so they cook in an even layer. Once the center is no longer runny, add half of each filling ingredient: pea tendrils, feta cheese, peas, avocado, and a pinch of red pepper flakes. Using a spatula, carefully fold the omelette in half and transfer to a plate. Season with salt and pepper.

Repeat, making a second omelette with the remaining ingredients.

NOTE Delicate pea tendrils, also known as pea shoots, aren't usually at a grocery store. Look for them at your farmers market at the beginning of spring.

GLUTEN-FREE

SERVES: **2**

PEA & SWEET POTATO SAMOSAS

DOUGH

¼ cup (60 mL) coconut oil

⅔ cup (150 mL) water

2 cups (500 mL) spelt flour or white/wheat mix, plus extra for working the dough

1 teaspoon (5 mL) sea salt

½ teaspoon (2 mL) baking powder

COCONUT CILANTRO CHUTNEY

½ cup (125 mL) light coconut milk or the water part of a full-fat can after solids are removed

¾ cup (180 mL) loosely packed cilantro

1 scallion, chopped

1 teaspoon (5 mL) grated ginger

1 small garlic clove

2 teaspoons (10 mL) olive oil

2 teaspoons (10 mL) fresh lemon juice

½ teaspoon (2 mL) honey

Sea salt and freshly ground black pepper

FILLING

1 medium sweet potato, chopped into small (¼-inch/0.5-cm) cubes (1½ cups/375 mL)

1 teaspoon (5 mL) sea salt

1 tablespoon (15 mL) extra-virgin olive oil

1 small yellow onion, chopped

2 teaspoons (10 mL) curry powder

¼ teaspoon (1 mL) cardamom

Pinch of red pepper flakes

2 garlic cloves, minced

½ cup (125 mL) peas, fresh or frozen

½ tablespoon (7 mL) fresh lemon juice

Coconut oil, for brushing

Sea salt and freshly ground black pepper

TIP: This recipe can also be made with store-bought wonton wrappers. Place 1 teaspoon of filling in each wrapper, dab water around the edges, fold in half, and press to seal. Bake until golden brown and crispy. Since they're smaller, this recipe will yield about 30 wonton pieces.

1 | Make the filling.

2 | Form and roll out the dough.

3 | Assemble samosas and bake.

4 | Serve with coconut cilantro chutney.

PEA & SWEET POTATO SAMOSAS

(CONTINUED)

Make the dough: In a small bowl, whisk together the coconut oil and water. In a larger bowl, combine the flour, salt, and baking powder. Stir two-thirds of the oil-water mixture into the dry flour ingredients, then add 1 tablespoon (15 mL) more at a time until you can form the dough into a ball. Transfer the dough to a lightly floured surface and knead for 1 minute. Form the dough into a ball and wrap it in plastic wrap. Let it rest at room temperature for 30 minutes.

Make the filling: Put the sweet potato cubes in a medium saucepan with the salt and cover with water. Bring to a boil over medium-high heat and cook for about 10 minutes, or until the potatoes are soft. Drain and set aside.

Heat the olive oil in a large skillet over medium heat. Add the onion and a pinch of salt and pepper and cook until the onion is soft and browned around the edges, about 5 minutes. Add the curry powder, cardamom, red pepper flakes, and garlic. Stir for 30 seconds, until the spices are aromatic. Add the sweet potatoes, peas, and a pinch of salt and pepper. Turn off the heat and stir in the lemon juice.

Preheat the oven to 375°F (190°C) and line a baking sheet with parchment paper.

Assemble the samosas: Working on a lightly floured surface, divide the dough into 4 equal pieces. Working one at a time, form each piece into a ball, flatten it out with your hand, and then roll it into an 8-inch (20-cm) disk. Dust with flour as needed. Cut the disk into quarters.

Add 1 tablespoon (15 mL) of filling to the center of one quarter. Fold one edge over to enclose the filling, and press to seal. Use a fork to crimp the sealed edges and secure the filling.

When all of the samosas are assembled, brush them liberally with coconut oil and bake for 30 to 35 minutes, or until crispy around the edges.

Make the coconut cilantro chutney: In a food processor, combine the coconut milk, cilantro, scallion, ginger, garlic, olive oil, lemon juice, and honey. Season with salt and pepper.

Yield: 16 pieces

VEGAN: Skip the honey and add a pinch of cane sugar.

SERVES: **4** *TO* **6**

20

PEPPERS

I attribute all of my healthy food tendencies to my mom. When my sister and I were younger, she didn't feed us refined sugar, chocolate, soda (we called it pop), or other junky things. She always told me how, when I was little, I would sit on the back stoop and eat a plate of sliced raw green peppers. When I became a Doritos-eating teenager, I hardly believed her. After college I shifted my eating habits and realized that if you're not eating processed food all that often, a bell pepper really does taste sweet.

SEASON

SUMMER

POBLANO QUESADILLAS

2 poblano peppers

4 whole wheat tortillas

2 cups (500 mL) shredded Monterey Jack cheese

2 cups (500 mL) baby spinach

¼ cup (60 mL) quick pickled onions (page 187)

1 small avocado, pitted and diced

Fresh lime juice

Handful of cilantro

Sea salt and freshly ground black pepper

Heat a cast-iron skillet or grill pan over medium-high heat. Place the peppers on the hot pan and use tongs to rotate them every few minutes until each side is lightly blackened. Alternatively, the peppers can be roasted under an oven broiler until charred. Remove the peppers from the heat, cut off the stems, remove the seeds, and dice.

Assemble each tortilla with the cheese, diced poblanos, spinach, pickled onions, and pinches of salt and pepper. Fold the tortillas in half and place in the hot skillet. Cook each side over medium heat for about 2 minutes, or until the tortillas are golden brown and the cheese is melted.

Toss the diced avocado with a squeeze of lime juice, a pinch of salt, and the cilantro. Serve on the side.

GLUTEN-FREE: Use corn tortillas.

SERVES: **4**

Nearly anything can go inside of a quesadilla, and it's fun to change up your filling. Roasted sweet potatoes, grilled mushrooms, roasted red peppers, zucchini, or black beans—you really can't mess this up!

ROASTED RED PEPPER & CARROT SOUP

2 tablespoons (30 mL) extra-virgin olive oil

1 medium yellow onion, chopped

2 garlic cloves, chopped

1 small fennel bulb, coarsely chopped

3 to 4 large carrots, chopped

1 tablespoon (15 mL) fresh thyme leaves

2 tablespoons (30 mL) balsamic vinegar

1 roasted red bell pepper, fresh or from a jar

¼ cup (60 mL) cooked cannellini beans, drained and rinsed (page 285)

2 tablespoons (30 mL) tomato paste

4 cups (1 L) vegetable broth

Sea salt and freshly ground black pepper

GARLIC CROUTONS

4 slices day-old bread, cubed

Extra-virgin olive oil, for drizzling

½ garlic clove, minced

Sea salt and freshly ground black pepper

Preheat the oven to 350°F (180°C).

Heat the olive oil in a large pot over medium heat. Add the onion and a pinch of salt and pepper and cook until translucent, about 5 minutes. Add the garlic, fennel, carrots, and thyme leaves. Stir and cook until the carrot edges begin to brown, about 10 minutes. Add the balsamic vinegar, bell pepper, cannellini beans, tomato paste, vegetable broth, and another few pinches of salt. Simmer until the carrots are tender, 15 to 20 minutes.

Meanwhile, make the croutons: On a baking sheet, toss the bread cubes with a drizzle of olive oil and the garlic. Season with salt and pepper. Bake until crispy, 10 to 15 minutes.

Add the simmered soup to a high-speed blender (you can work in batches if you need to) and puree until smooth. Taste and adjust the seasonings.

Serve in bowls with a drizzle of olive oil and the croutons on top.

VEGAN | **GLUTEN-FREE:** Skip the croutons. | *SERVES:* **4**

RED PEPPER FETA FRITTATA

6 large eggs

¼ cup (60 mL) almond milk

½ teaspoon (2 mL) coconut oil

1 roasted red bell pepper, fresh or from a jar, chopped

2 cups (500 mL) spinach

⅓ cup (75 mL) crumbled feta cheese

¼ teaspoon (1 mL) red pepper flakes

Sea salt and freshly ground black pepper

Preheat the oven to 400°F (200°C) with an 8-inch (20-cm) cast-iron skillet inside.

In a medium bowl, whisk the eggs with the almond milk and a few pinches of salt and pepper.

Using a pot holder, remove the preheated skillet from the oven and add the coconut oil to coat the bottom. Pour in the egg mixture, followed by the bell peppers, spinach, and feta cheese. Bake until the eggs are set and the frittata is golden brown on top, 15 to 20 minutes.

Remove the frittata from the oven, sprinkle with the red pepper flakes, and season with black pepper. Let cool slightly and serve.

NOTE ½ cup (125 mL) chopped raw red bell pepper can be substituted for the roasted pepper.

GLUTEN-FREE

SERVES: **2**

Whether you make them for breakfast, brunch, or dinner, frittatas are always a crowd favorite as well as a great opportunity to clean out the fridge. This red bell pepper, spinach, and feta cheese version is pretty simple, but if you have scallions, summer squash, or tomatoes to use up—pile them in.

These peppers
are generally
mild in flavor,
but "they" say
every 1 in 10
peppers is a
spicy one. The
fun of eating
these is that it's
a game of hot-
pepper roulette!

BLISTERED PADRÓN PEPPERS

2 cups (500 mL) padrón peppers
(or shishito peppers)

Toasted sesame oil, for drizzling

Sea salt

1 teaspoon (5 mL) sesame seeds

Preheat a 10-inch (25-cm) or larger cast-iron skillet under the broiler, or at your oven's highest temperature.

Once the skillet is hot, use a pot holder to remove it from the oven.

Place the peppers on the dry skillet and roast for 20 to 25 minutes, flipping halfway through, until golden brown.

Remove the peppers from the oven, transfer to a plate, and drizzle with sesame oil. Add a pinch of salt and sprinkle with the sesame seeds.

VEGAN | **GLUTEN-FREE**

SERVES: **4**

GRILLED PEPPER
& QUINOA TACO SALAD

INGREDIENTS

2 corn tortillas, sliced into thin strips

Extra-virgin olive oil, for drizzling

Sea salt

4 Anaheim or bell peppers

1½ cups (375 mL) cooked quinoa (page 284)

1½ cups (375 mL) cooked black beans, drained and rinsed (page 285)

2 radishes, thinly sliced

1 cup (250 mL) halved cherry tomatoes

¼ cup (60 mL) pepitas

1 avocado, pitted and diced

Lime slices for serving

1 jalapeño, sliced (optional)

DRESSING

2 tablespoons (30 mL) extra-virgin olive oil

1 tablespoon (15 mL) fresh lime juice, plus more to taste

¼ teaspoon (1 mL) maple syrup or honey

½ teaspoon (2 mL) cumin

½ teaspoon (2 mL) coriander

1 teaspoon (5 mL) chili powder

Sea salt and freshly ground black pepper

1 recipe chili-spiced yogurt (page 287)

DIRECTIONS

Preheat the oven to 350°F (180°C). Line a baking sheet with parchment paper. Add the tortilla strips to the baking sheet and toss with a drizzle of olive oil and a pinch of salt. Bake for 12 minutes, or until crispy. Remove from the oven and set aside.

Heat a grill or grill pan to medium-high heat. Place the peppers on the grill or grill pan and use tongs to rotate them every few minutes until each side is lightly blackened, about 10 minutes. Remove the peppers from the heat and let cool for several minutes. Slice off the stems and remove any loose, blistered skin. Cut the peppers in half vertically, remove the seeds, and slice in ¼-inch (0.5-cm) strips.

Make the dressing: In a small bowl, whisk together the olive oil, lime juice, maple syrup, cumin, coriander, chili powder, and a pinch of salt and pepper.

Assemble the salad: In a large bowl, combine the peppers with the quinoa, black beans, radishes, cherry tomatoes, pepitas, and jalapeño, if using. Pour the dressing over the salad. Gently mix in the avocado and top with the baked tortilla strips. Season with more salt, pepper, and lime juice to taste.

Serve with the chili-spiced yogurt and the lime slices.

VEGAN: Use sun "cheese" (page 286) to make the chili-spiced yogurt and skip the honey.

GLUTEN-FREE

SERVES: **4**

21

POTATOES

I love roasted or fried potatoes as much as the next person,
but I think of white potatoes as more of a "sometimes" treat.
Sweet potatoes, on the other hand, are an everyday staple for me
through the fall and winter. I roast sweet potato cubes and put them
in everything from salads to tacos to baked eggs. I've also discovered
that sweet potatoes are a great healthy treat for your dog.

SEASON

VARIES

SWEET POTATO TACOS
WITH APPLE RADISH SLAW

INGREDIENTS

2 medium sweet potatoes, cubed
(about 1½ pounds/700 g)

2 teaspoons (10 mL) extra-virgin olive oil

½ teaspoon (2 mL) chili powder

8 tortillas, warmed or grilled

1 recipe apple radish slaw (page 11)

1 avocado, diced

Lime wedges for serving

Sea salt and freshly ground black pepper

DIRECTIONS

Preheat the oven to 400°F (200°C). Line a large baking sheet with parchment paper. Toss the sweet potatoes with the olive oil, chili powder, and pinches of salt and pepper. Roast until golden brown, about 25 minutes.

Fill each tortilla with the sweet potatoes, apple radish slaw, and diced avocado. Serve with lime wedges.

VEGAN | **GLUTEN-FREE:** Use corn tortillas. | *SERVES:* **4**

BAKED EGGS WITH KALE, SAGE & SWEET POTATOES

1 small sweet potato, chopped into ¾-inch (2-cm) cubes

Extra-virgin olive oil, for drizzling and brushing

¼ teaspoon (1 mL) smoked paprika

3 kale leaves, chopped

6 sage leaves, chopped

4 large eggs

¼ cup (60 mL) crumbled feta cheese

1 tablespoon (15 mL) chopped chives

Sea salt and freshly ground black pepper

Preheat the oven to 400°F (200°C). Line a baking sheet with parchment paper.

Spread the sweet potato cubes on the baking sheet. Drizzle with olive oil, smoked paprika, and a pinch of salt and pepper and toss to combine. Roast until golden brown, about 25 minutes. Remove from the oven and reduce the oven heat to 300°F (150°C).

Brush the bottoms of two mini-skillets or ramekins with olive oil. Add the kale, sage, and roasted sweet potatoes. Crack 2 eggs on top of each skillet and sprinkle with feta cheese. Bake for 15 to 20 minutes, or until the eggs have set but the yolks are still runny. Top with the chives and pinches of salt and pepper.

GLUTEN-FREE

SERVES: **2**

1	Wash the potatoes and slice them in half.
2	Make the dressing and mix it with the potatoes. Spread them on a baking sheet.

3	Roast the potatoes, then toss with the remaining dressing and fresh parsley.
4	Grate some fresh lemon zest on the potatoes and serve hot!

LEMON ROSEMARY
ROASTED POTATOES

2 tablespoons (30 mL) extra-virgin olive oil

Juice and zest of 1 small lemon

1 teaspoon (5 mL) Dijon mustard

1 tablespoon (15 mL) minced rosemary

¼ teaspoon (1 mL) red pepper flakes

1½ pounds (700 g) small creamer or fingerling potatoes

¼ cup (60 mL) chopped flat-leaf parsley

Sea salt and freshly ground black pepper

Preheat the oven to 400°F (200°C) and line a baking sheet with parchment paper.

In a small bowl, whisk together the olive oil, lemon juice, Dijon mustard, rosemary, red pepper flakes, and generous pinches of salt and pepper.

Slice the potatoes into wedges, place them in a medium bowl, and toss with half of the dressing. Spread the potatoes on the baking sheet. Roast for 20 minutes. Toss, and continue roasting, until the potatoes are golden brown and crispy on the edges, 5 to 10 minutes longer.

Remove the potatoes from the oven and toss with the remaining dressing, lemon zest, and chopped parsley. Season with salt and pepper to taste.

VEGAN | **GLUTEN-FREE**

SERVES: **4**

LOADED SWEET POTATO NACHOS

2 sweet potatoes, thinly sliced

Extra-virgin olive oil, for drizzling

1 cup (250 mL) shredded Monterey
Jack cheese

1 cup (250 mL) cooked black beans, drained
and rinsed (page 285)

1 mango, peeled and diced

3 radishes, sliced

1 avocado, diced

1 serrano pepper, thinly sliced

1 small lime, sliced into wedges

¼ cup (60 mL) adobo sauce from canned
chipotles in adobo sauce

Sea salt and freshly ground black pepper

Preheat the oven to 400°F (200°C) and line
a large baking sheet with parchment paper.

Toss the sweet potatoes with a drizzle of
olive oil and a pinch of salt and pepper.
Spread in a thin layer on the baking sheet
and bake for 15 minutes. Top with the
cheese and bake for an additional
10 minutes, or until the cheese is melted
and the sweet potatoes are golden brown.

Remove the baking sheet from the oven and
top the sweet potatoes with the black beans,
mango, radishes, avocado, and serrano
pepper. Add a squeeze of lime, drizzle with
the adobo sauce, and sprinkle with a few
pinches of salt. Serve straight from the pan
with extra lime slices on the side.

TIP Use a mandoline, if you have one, to slice the sweet potatoes into thin,
uniform slices so that they cook evenly.

GLUTEN-FREE

SERVES: **4** *AS AN APPETIZER*

SCARLET
TURNIPS

BLACK RADISHES

RADISHES

TOKYO TURNIPS

WATERMELON RADISHES

22

ROOT

VEGGIES

Radishes and turnips aren't always on my grocery list, but when I'm shopping at farm stands, I'm inexplicably drawn to them. In the gray of winter, hot pink scarlet turnips find their way into my bag every time. Black radishes look daunting, but when sliced paper-thin, their white translucency is stunning on a salad. My favorite is the watermelon radish—it's the most unassuming vegetable on the outside, but so gorgeous on the inside, with its hot pink and green center.

SEASON

VARIES

CURRIED PARSNIP
& WHITE BEAN SOUP

3 tablespoons (45 mL) extra-virgin olive oil

1 medium yellow onion, chopped

3 garlic cloves, minced

1 teaspoon (5 mL) freshly grated ginger

5 to 6 medium parsnips, peeled and chopped

1 Gala apple, peeled, cored, and chopped

1 teaspoon (5 mL) curry powder

½ teaspoon (2 mL) ground cardamom

1½ cups (375 mL) cooked cannellini beans, drained and rinsed (page 285), ¼ cup (60 mL) reserved for garnish

4 cups (1 L) vegetable broth

¼ cup (60 mL) chopped chives

Sea salt and freshly ground black pepper

In a large pot, heat the olive oil over medium heat. Add the onion and a few generous pinches of salt and pepper and cook until soft, about 2 minutes.

Add the garlic and ginger and stir. Add the parsnips, apple, curry powder, cardamom, and cannellini beans. Stir and cook until the parsnips are lightly browned, about 2 minutes. Add the vegetable broth and simmer until the parsnips are tender, about 20 minutes.

Let the soup cool slightly, then transfer it to a blender (you can work in batches if you need to) and puree until creamy.

Season with more salt and pepper to taste. Garnish with the reserved cannellini beans and chopped chives.

VEGAN | **GLUTEN-FREE**

SERVES: **4**

KALE SALAD WITH ROASTED ROOT VEGGIES

1 medium sweet potato, chopped into 1-inch (2.5-cm) cubes

2 small radishes, quartered

2 turnips, chopped

1 teaspoon (5 mL) + 1 tablespoon (15 mL) extra-virgin olive oil

1 tablespoon (15 mL) chopped rosemary

1 bunch of kale

1 medium orange, ½ juiced, ½ cut into segments

1 teaspoon (5 mL) white wine vinegar

½ cup (125 mL) cooked chickpeas, drained and rinsed (page 285)

¼ cup (60 mL) crumbled feta cheese

¼ cup (60 mL) sliced shallots

¼ cup (60 mL) hemp seeds, sunflower seeds, or pine nuts, toasted (page 285)

Pinch of red pepper flakes

Sea salt and freshly ground black pepper

DIRECTIONS

Preheat the oven to 400°F (200°C) and line a baking sheet with parchment paper.

Place the sweet potatoes, radishes, and turnips on the baking sheet and toss with 1 teaspoon (5 mL) of olive oil, the rosemary, and a few pinches of salt and pepper. Roast for 30 to 35 minutes, or until golden brown on the edges.

Tear the kale into 1-inch (2.5-cm) pieces, removing the coarse stems. Place the kale in a large bowl and drizzle with 1 tablespoon (15 mL) of olive oil. Add the orange juice, white wine vinegar, and a pinch of salt and pepper. Massage the leaves until they soften and wilt down. Add the orange segments, chickpeas, feta cheese, shallots, seeds or nuts, and red pepper flakes and toss. Set aside.

Let the roasted veggies cool for a few minutes and then toss them into the salad. Season to taste.

VEGAN: Skip the cheese. | **GLUTEN-FREE** | *SERVES:* **4**

PARSNIP FRIES WITH
RED PEPPER HUMMUS

INGREDIENTS

1 bunch of parsnips, about 1 pound (450 g)

Extra-virgin olive oil, for drizzling

¼ cup (60 mL) chopped parsley

Sea salt and freshly ground black pepper

- -

RED PEPPER HUMMUS

1½ cups (375 mL) cooked chickpeas, drained and rinsed (page 285)

1 small garlic clove

2 tablespoons (30 mL) fresh lemon juice

1 roasted red bell pepper, fresh or from a jar

¼ cup (60 mL) almonds, toasted (page 285)

½ teaspoon (2 mL) smoked paprika

¼ cup (60 mL) extra-virgin olive oil

Sea salt and freshly ground black pepper

DIRECTIONS

Preheat the oven to 350°F (180°C). Line a large baking sheet with parchment paper.

Scrub the parsnips and slice into thin strips. Toss with a drizzle of olive oil and a few generous pinches of salt and pepper. Roast for 20 to 25 minutes, flipping halfway through, until golden brown.

Make the red pepper hummus: In a food processor, combine the chickpeas, garlic, lemon juice, bell pepper, almonds, smoked paprika, olive oil, and pinches of salt and pepper. Blend until smooth. Add 2 to 3 tablespoons (30 to 45 mL) of warm water for a smooth consistency. Chill until ready to use.

Remove the parsnips from the oven, toss with the parsley, and serve with the red pepper hummus for dipping. They're best served hot.

.TIP Can't find parsnips? Make sweet potato fries instead!

VEGAN | **GLUTEN-FREE** *SERVES:* **4**

The fun of a CSA vegetable box is in the unexpected. The first time I received kohlrabi, I had no clue what to do with this alien vegetable. Since then, I've grown to love its crunch when thinly sliced and tossed into slaws and noodle salads and wrapped into these spring rolls.

KOHLRABI SPRING ROLLS

PEANUT DIPPING SAUCE

⅓ cup (75 mL) creamy peanut butter

2 teaspoons (10 mL) tamari, plus more
to taste

Juice of ½ lime, plus more to taste

2 to 3 tablespoons (30 to 45 mL) water

1 teaspoon (5 mL) sriracha, plus more
to taste

¼ cup (60 mL) crushed peanuts, toasted
(page 285)

- -

4 ounces (115 g) vermicelli rice noodles

1 kohlrabi bulb, sliced into matchsticks

Juice of ½ lime

1 mango, peeled and sliced into thin strips

1 avocado, pitted and sliced

½ cup (125 mL) loosely packed basil

½ cup (125 mL) loosely packed mint

8 rice papers

Sea salt

¼ cup (60 mL) microgreens (optional)

Make the peanut dipping sauce: In a small
bowl, mix together the peanut butter,
tamari, lime juice, water, and sriracha.
Taste and adjust the seasonings. Sprinkle
with crushed peanuts.

Bring a large pot of water to a boil.
Prepare the vermicelli rice noodles
according to the instructions on the
package. Drain and set aside.

Toss the sliced kohlrabi with the lime
juice and a pinch of salt. Have all filling
ingredients prepped and in front of
you before you start rolling—noodles,
kohlrabi, mango, avocado, basil, mint,
and microgreens, if using.

Assemble the spring rolls: Fill a shallow
glass baking dish or pie plate with 1 inch
(2.5 cm) of warm water. Submerge one rice
paper wrapper in the warm water for
15 seconds and then lay the softened
wrapper on a clean kitchen towel. Place a
portion of each filling ingredient on the
rice paper. Fold the bottom of the wrapper
over the filling and gently tuck the filling
under the wrapper. Fold the sides over the
filling. Then continue rolling and tucking
the rice paper to form the spring roll.
Repeat with the remaining rice papers.

Serve with the peanut dipping sauce.

VEGAN | **GLUTEN-FREE**

SERVES: **4**

SPRING POLENTA WITH RADISHES & GARLIC SCAPES

POLENTA

3 cups (750 mL) water

1 cup (250 mL) polenta

1 garlic clove, minced

2 tablespoons (30 mL) extra-virgin olive oil or unsalted butter

Sea salt and freshly ground black pepper

¼ cup (60 mL) grated pecorino cheese (optional)

- -

1 teaspoon (5 mL) extra-virgin olive oil

12 radishes, sliced in half

1 cup (250 mL) cooked chickpeas, drained and rinsed (page 285)

3 garlic scapes, sliced into 1-inch (2.5-cm) pieces (about 1 cup/250 mL)

2 cups (500 mL) broccolini

Radish sprouts

Sea salt

Make the polenta: In a medium saucepan, bring the water to a boil over medium-high heat. Add a few generous pinches of salt. Gradually whisk in the polenta and bring back to a boil. Reduce the heat and continue cooking until the polenta is tender, 20 to 30 minutes, whisking often. Turn off the heat and whisk in the garlic, olive oil or butter, pinches of salt and pepper, and cheese, if using. Taste and adjust the seasonings. Cover to keep warm.

In a large skillet, heat the olive oil over medium heat. Add the radishes, chickpeas, and a pinch of salt and sauté for 5 minutes. Stir, then add the garlic scapes and broccolini and cook until the vegetables are tender but still have a vibrant bite, about 5 more minutes. Season with salt and pepper. Spoon the polenta into bowls and top with the vegetables and radish sprouts.

VEGAN | **GLUTEN-FREE**

SERVES: **4**

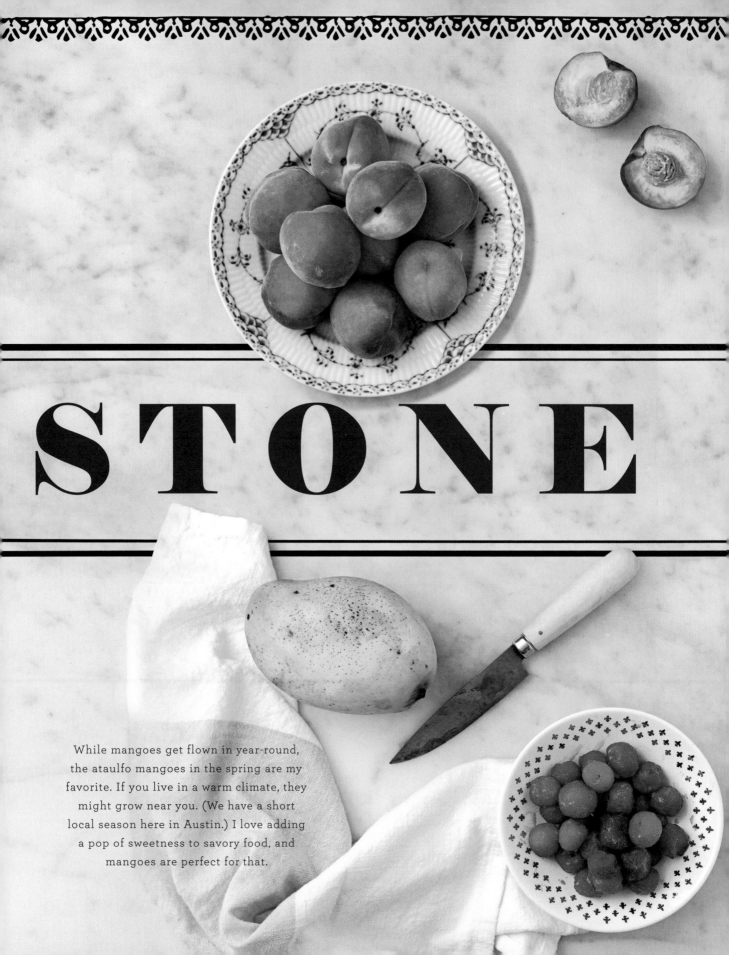

STONE

While mangoes get flown in year-round, the ataulfo mangoes in the spring are my favorite. If you live in a warm climate, they might grow near you. (We have a short local season here in Austin.) I love adding a pop of sweetness to savory food, and mangoes are perfect for that.

23

FRUITS

I don't care what the calendar says: The first day of summer for me is the day I bite into my first Texas peach of the year and feel the juices dripping down my elbow. The only problem with peaches is that they go from underripe to overripe really quickly. While I have eaten a basket of peaches in one day, I prefer to have some handy recipes ready for when I have too many ripe peaches. Peach salsa, grilled peach salad, and peach pizza are some of my favorites.

SEASON

SUMMER

This is a version of the most popular recipe on loveandlemons.com. Whether you're vegan, or you've just run out of eggs, this tastes like the real thing. We like ours smothered with maple syrup and tart cherries.

VEGAN TART CHERRY FRENCH TOAST

1⅓ cups (325 mL) almond milk

¼ cup (60 mL) spelt or whole wheat flour

1 tablespoon (15 mL) maple syrup, plus more for serving

1 tablespoon (15 mL) almond butter

1 tablespoon + 1 teaspoon (20 mL) nutritional yeast

1 teaspoon (5 mL) cinnamon

¼ teaspoon (1 mL) freshly ground nutmeg

⅛ teaspoon (0.5 mL) sea salt

8 slices day-old ciabatta bread, sliced about ¾ inch (2 cm) thick

Coconut oil, for drizzling

TOPPINGS

Coconut cream (page 287)

Tart cherries (thawed if frozen)

Pomegranate seeds

In a small bowl, whisk together the almond milk, flour, maple syrup, almond butter, nutritional yeast, cinnamon, nutmeg, and salt.

Place the bread in a shallow baking dish that's large enough to hold the bread in a single layer. Pour the almond milk mixture over the bread, then lift or flip the bread over to make sure both sides are evenly coated.

In a large skillet, heat a drizzle of coconut oil over medium heat. When the pan is hot, add the bread slices in a single layer and cook for a few minutes per side, or until golden brown. Repeat with any remaining slices.

Serve with the coconut cream, tart cherries, pomegranate seeds, and maple syrup.

VEGAN

SERVES: 4

MANGO & DAIKON
GLASS NOODLE SALAD

DRESSING

1 tablespoon (15 mL) tamari

1 garlic clove, minced

1 tablespoon (15 mL) fresh lime juice

1 tablespoon (15 mL) rice vinegar

2 teaspoons (10 mL) cane sugar

- -

1 unripe mango, peeled and thinly sliced

2 daikon, peeled into ribbons

1 carrot, peeled into ribbons

4 ounces (115 g) rice vermicelli noodles

¼ cup (60 mL) chopped mint

¼ cup (60 mL) chopped basil

½ cup (125 mL) chopped cilantro

¼ cup (60 mL) microgreens, for garnish

¼ cup (60 mL) crushed peanuts, toasted (page 285)

½ teaspoon (2 mL) sriracha, or to taste

Lime wedges, for serving

Sea salt

Make the dressing: In a small bowl, whisk together the tamari, garlic, lime juice, rice vinegar, and sugar.

In a large bowl, toss together the mango, daikon, and carrot. Drizzle in half of the dressing and toss. Chill for 15 minutes.

Meanwhile, prepare the rice noodles according to the instructions on the package. Drain and rinse with cold water.

Add the noodles to the salad bowl along with the remaining dressing, mint, basil, and cilantro and toss with a few pinches of salt to taste. Top with the microgreens, toasted peanuts, and sriracha to taste. Serve with lime wedges.

VEGAN | **GLUTEN-FREE**

SERVES: **4**

FARM STAND PEACH PIZZAS

INGREDIENTS

4 pieces pita bread or naan

1 cup (250 mL) shredded white cheddar cheese

½ zucchini, thinly sliced into coins

8 squash blossoms

½ cup (125 mL) halved cherry tomatoes

3 ripe peaches, sliced into segments

½ cup (125 mL) crumbled feta cheese

Extra-virgin olive oil, for drizzling

Fresh herbs (a few basil or oregano leaves)

½ teaspoon (2 mL) red pepper flakes

Sea salt and freshly ground black pepper

DIRECTIONS

Preheat the oven to 350°F (180°C) and line a baking sheet with parchment paper.

Assemble the pita bread or naan with the white cheddar cheese, zucchini, squash blossoms, cherry tomatoes, peaches, and feta cheese. Bake until the cheese is golden brown and the peaches and zucchini are tender, about 15 minutes.

Remove from the oven, drizzle with olive oil, and top with the fresh herbs and red pepper flakes. Season with salt and pepper to taste.

VEGAN: Skip the cheese and top with one of the vegan pestos on page 275.

SERVES: **4** *AS AN APPETIZER*

GRILLED PEACH SALAD WITH TOASTED PISTACHIOS

INGREDIENTS

4 to 6 ripe peaches

Extra-virgin olive oil, for drizzling

3 cups (750 mL) watercress leaves

8 ounces (225 g) medium-size fresh mozzarella balls, sliced

⅓ cup (75 mL) pistachios, toasted and chopped (page 285)

Sea salt and freshly ground black pepper

¼ teaspoon (1 mL) red pepper flakes (optional)

DIRECTIONS

Heat a grill or grill pan to medium heat. Slice the peaches into segments and drizzle with olive oil and a few pinches of salt. Grill for 1 to 2 minutes per side, or until char marks form.

Remove from the heat and assemble the salad with the watercress, mozzarella slices, peaches, pistachios, and red pepper flakes, if using. Season with salt and pepper and drizzle with olive oil.

TIP If using a grill pan, it's handy to use a nonstick pan for this one.

VEGAN: Use avocado slices instead of cheese.

GLUTEN-FREE

SERVES: **4**

TIP: Avoid storing tomatoes in the fridge; they'll lose all their flavor. Keep them on your countertop instead. They're also pretty to look at!

24

Tomatoes

I've always loved tomatoes. Sliced, sauced, etc. . . . I wasn't picky, I just
liked them. But my first trip to Italy ruined me for every tomato that
would come after. Jack and I spent time on the island of Capri, where the
tomatoes are the sweetest and most flavorful I've ever had. Back home,
I still appreciate a good just-picked tomato, but only in the summer.

SEASON

SUMMER

TOMATO CHICKPEA TORTILLA SOUP

4 corn tortillas, sliced into thin strips

1 tablespoon (15 mL) extra-virgin olive oil, plus more for drizzling and brushing

2½ pounds (1.25 kg) tomatoes (6 medium tomatoes on the vine)

1 ear of fresh corn, husked

1 small red onion, diced, ¼ cup (60 mL) reserved for topping

2 garlic cloves, minced

1 teaspoon (5 mL) cumin

1 teaspoon (5 mL) coriander

¼ teaspoon (1 mL) cane sugar

2 tablespoons (30 mL) adobo sauce from canned chipotles in adobo sauce

2 cups (500 mL) vegetable broth

1 cup (250 mL) cooked chickpeas, drained and rinsed (page 285)

Sea salt and freshly ground black pepper

TOPPINGS

Diced red onion

Avocado slices

Lime slices

Serrano or jalapeño pepper, sliced (optional)

Preheat the oven to 350°F (180°C). Line a baking sheet with parchment paper. Add the tortilla strips to the baking sheet and toss with a drizzle of olive oil and a pinch of salt. Bake for 12 minutes, or until crispy. Remove from the oven and set aside.

Heat a medium cast-iron skillet or grill pan over medium heat. Place the whole tomatoes on the hot dry skillet. Rotate every few minutes until they are nicely charred on all sides, the skins start to break open, and the tomatoes have softened, 10 to 12 minutes. Transfer to a plate to cool, then remove the core of the tomatoes.

Brush the ear of corn with a bit of olive oil, sprinkle lightly with salt, and place on the hot skillet. Cook for 10 minutes, or until nicely charred on all sides. Set aside to cool, then slice the kernels from the cob.

Heat 1 tablespoon (15 mL) of olive oil in a large pot over medium-low heat. Add the onion and a pinch of salt and pepper and sauté for 5 minutes, or until the onion is translucent. Stir in the garlic, cumin, and coriander. Use your hands to crush the tomatoes into the pot, then use a masher to break them up more. Add the sugar and stir. Stir in the adobo sauce, vegetable broth, and chickpeas. Cover and simmer for 20 minutes. Add in the corn kernels. Taste and adjust the seasonings.

Top the soup with the crispy tortilla strips, and serve with the diced red onion, avocado slices, lime slices, and serrano pepper, if using.

VEGAN | GLUTEN-FREE

SERVES: **4**

GREEN TOMATO BASIL GRILLED CHEESE

INGREDIENTS

2 green tomatoes

8 slices sourdough bread

1 tablespoon (15 mL) grainy mustard

3 cups (750 mL) grated Gruyère cheese

Handful of fresh basil leaves

Extra-virgin olive oil, for brushing on bread

Sea salt and freshly ground black pepper

DIRECTIONS

Slice the tomatoes into ¼-inch (0.5-cm) slices. Set on a plate and season with salt and pepper.

Assemble 4 slices of bread with a slather of mustard and top with half of the cheese. Add 1 to 2 basil leaves, 2 to 3 tomato slices, and the remaining cheese. Top with the remaining slices of bread and brush both sides of the sandwich with olive oil.

Heat a grill pan or large skillet over medium heat. Grill the sandwiches about 5 minutes per side, or until the bread is golden brown and the cheese is melted, pressing down with a spatula or another pan to help melt the cheese.

NOTE White cheddar, smoked mozzarella, or even vegan Daiya cheese would work well in place of Gruyère.

SERVES: **4**

HEIRLOOM TOMATO PANZANELLA WITH FRESH OREGANO

1 pound (450 g) heirloom tomatoes, cored and sliced into wedges

¼ red onion, thinly sliced

2 tablespoons (30 mL) sherry vinegar

1 tablespoon (15 mL) extra-virgin olive oil, plus more for drizzling

6 thick slices whole-grain bread or ciabatta bread

½ garlic clove

½ cup (125 mL) fresh basil, torn

½ cup (125 mL) fresh oregano

Sea salt and freshly ground black pepper

In a large bowl, combine the tomatoes and the red onion slices with the sherry vinegar, olive oil, and pinches of salt and pepper.

Heat a grill or grill pan to medium heat. Drizzle the bread slices with olive oil and place on the hot grill. Cook 1 to 2 minutes on each side, until grill marks form. Remove from the heat and rub the warm grilled bread with the cut side of the garlic clove. Slice the bread into 1-inch (2.5-cm) cubes.

Place the bread cubes in the bowl with the tomatoes and onion. Add the basil, oregano, and a few pinches of salt and pepper, and toss to coat. Add a drizzle of olive oil, if desired. Let sit 10 minutes before serving.

VEGAN

SERVES: **4**

I typically use only basil in my panzanella, but one day my herb garden was overflowing with oregano, and I loved this unexpected (accidental) twist. Feel free to experiment with any soft leafy herbs you might have.

1 Rinse 3 pounds of tomatoes.

2 Char tomatoes on all sides.

3 Crush tomatoes into the pot with olive oil, minced shallot and garlic.

4 Simmer and season to taste.

SIMPLE FRESH TOMATO SAUCE

INGREDIENTS	DIRECTIONS
3 pounds (1.36 kg) tomatoes on the vine	Heat a medium cast-iron skillet or grill pan over medium heat. Place the whole tomatoes on the hot skillet. Rotate every few minutes until nicely charred on all sides, the tomato skins start to break open, and the tomatoes have softened, 12 to 15 minutes. Transfer to a plate to cool, then remove the core of the tomatoes.
3 tablespoons (45 mL) extra-virgin olive oil	
1 small shallot, minced	
2 large garlic cloves, minced	
2 teaspoons (10 mL) balsamic vinegar	
½ teaspoon (2 mL) raw cane sugar	
½ teaspoon (2 mL) red pepper flakes	
Sea salt and freshly ground black pepper	Heat the olive oil in a large pot or Dutch oven over low heat. Add the minced shallot, garlic, and pinches of salt and pepper and cook for about 3 minutes. Use your hands to crush the tomatoes into the pot, then use a masher to break them up more. Stir, then add the balsamic vinegar, sugar, and red pepper flakes.
	Simmer over low heat for 20 minutes. Season with more salt and black pepper to taste.
	Yield: 3 cups

NOTE — If you would like a smoother sauce, use a food mill to remove the seeds and skins before adding the tomatoes to the pot. Or blend the finished sauce.

VEGAN | **GLUTEN-FREE**

25

WINTER SQUASH

Butternut, delicata, kabocha, acorn, buttercup, red kuri,
and, of course, the ever pinnable pumpkin. Chop them and roast
them, stuff them, puree them, or pie them.

SEASON

WINTER

WHEAT BERRY DELICATA SQUASH SALAD

INGREDIENTS

2 small delicata squash or a 1-pound (450-g) butternut squash

1 tablespoon (15 mL) extra-virgin olive oil, plus more for drizzling

Maple syrup, for drizzling

1 bunch of kale

Juice of ½ medium orange

Juice of ½ lemon

2 cups (500 mL) arugula

1 cup (250 mL) cooked hard or soft wheat berries (page 284)

1 apple, cored and thinly sliced

⅓ cup (75 mL) dried cranberries

½ cup (125 mL) shaved pecorino cheese

Sea salt and freshly ground black pepper

DIRECTIONS

Preheat the oven to 400°F (200°C). Line a baking sheet with parchment paper.

Cut the delicata squash in half lengthwise and scoop out the seeds. Slice into 1-inch (2.5-cm) segments and place on the baking sheet. Drizzle with olive oil and maple syrup. Season with pinches of salt and pepper and toss. Roast the squash for 18 to 25 minutes, or until tender and golden brown on the edges.

Tear the kale into 1-inch (2.5-cm) pieces and remove the coarse stems. Place the kale in a large bowl and drizzle with 1 tablespoon (15 mL) of olive oil. Add the orange and lemon juices and a pinch of salt and pepper. Massage the kale leaves until they soften and wilt down. Add the arugula, cooked wheat berries, apple slices, cranberries, and cheese. Toss to combine, then taste and adjust the seasonings.

Top the salad with the roasted delicata squash and serve.

VEGAN: Skip the cheese. | **GLUTEN-FREE:** Use quinoa instead of wheat berries. | *SERVES:* 4

BUTTERNUT SQUASH RED CURRY

3 tablespoons (45 mL) coconut oil

1 medium yellow onion, chopped

4 cups (1 L) cubed butternut squash

4 garlic cloves, minced

1 to 2 tablespoons (15 to 30 mL) red curry paste

1 cup (250 mL) canned or fresh diced tomatoes

2 (14-ounce/414-mL) cans light coconut milk

12 ounces (340 g) extra-firm tofu, patted dry and cubed

4 cups (1 L) baby spinach

Juice of 1 small lime

2 cups (500 mL) cooked quinoa (page 284)

Sea salt and freshly ground black pepper

In a large pot over medium heat, heat 2 tablespoons (30 mL) of coconut oil. Add the onion and season with a pinch of salt and pepper. Cook for about 5 minutes, then add the cubed butternut squash. Cook until the onion is soft and the butternut squash is beginning to brown around the edges, about 10 minutes.

Add the garlic and red curry paste and stir. Then add the tomatoes, coconut milk, and another pinch of salt. Stir, then reduce the heat to low. Simmer for 15 minutes, or until the butternut squash is tender.

Meanwhile, in a large skillet, heat the remaining 1 tablespoon (15 mL) of coconut oil over medium heat. Add the cubed tofu in a single layer and sear each side for 1 to 2 minutes, or until golden brown, about 6 minutes total.

Add the spinach to the butternut squash curry and stir until wilted, 1 to 2 minutes. Add the lime juice and the seared tofu. Taste and adjust the seasonings.

Serve with quinoa.

VEGAN | **GLUTEN-FREE**

SERVES: **4** *TO* **6**

1 Peel, chop, and roast the butternut squash.

2 Mix the squash with black beans and scallions and make the enchilada sauce.

3 Assemble the enchiladas.

4 Cover the enchiladas with sauce and cheese and bake until the cheese bubbles.

BUTTERNUT SQUASH
& BLACK BEAN ENCHILADAS

FILLING

2 cups (500 mL) cubed butternut squash

Extra-virgin olive oil, for drizzling

⅓ cup (75 mL) chopped scallions

1 cup (250 mL) cooked black beans, drained and rinsed (page 285)

Sea salt and freshly ground black pepper

SAUCE

1 can (14.5 ounces/411 g) diced tomatoes

1 garlic clove

1 chipotle pepper from canned chipotles in adobo sauce

2 teaspoons (10 mL) extra-virgin olive oil

Sea salt and freshly ground black pepper

6 corn tortillas

2 cups (500 mL) grated cheddar cheese

1 jalapeño, sliced

Cilantro, for garnish

Avocado slices

Lime slices

Preheat the oven to 400°F (200°C). Line a baking sheet with parchment paper.

Make the filling: Spread the butternut squash cubes on the baking sheet. Drizzle with olive oil, add a pinch of salt and pepper, and toss to combine. Roast until golden brown, about 25 minutes. Transfer the roasted squash to a bowl and stir in the scallions and black beans.

Make the sauce: In a food processor, blend the tomatoes, garlic, chipotle pepper, olive oil, and pinches of salt and pepper until smooth. In a 9 x 13-inch (23 x 33-cm) baking dish, spread 2 tablespoons (30 mL) of the sauce on the bottom of the dish. Assemble the corn tortillas with about ½ cup (125 mL) of the filling, a tablespoon (15 mL) of the sauce, and a sprinkle of cheese. Roll each tortilla and place seam side down in the baking dish.

Pour the remaining sauce over the enchiladas and sprinkle with the remaining cheese and the jalapeño slices. Bake, covered, for 20 minutes. Uncover and bake for 5 more minutes, or until the cheese is bubbling.

Serve with fresh cilantro, avocado slices, and lime slices.

VEGAN: Skip the cheese and serve chipotle sun "cheese" (page 286) on the side.

GLUTEN-FREE

SERVES: **3**

CREAMY PUMPKIN
BROWN RICE PENNE

½ kabocha or small sugar pie pumpkin (yield 1 heaping cup/250 mL of cooked mash)

½ yellow onion sliced into wedges

2 garlic cloves, unpeeled

Extra-virgin olive oil, for drizzling

5 fresh sage leaves

¾ cup (175 mL) vegetable broth

½ cup (125 mL) raw unsalted cashews, soaked 3 to 4 hours, preferably overnight, drained and rinsed

2 tablespoons (30 mL) extra-virgin olive oil

16 ounces (450 g) uncooked brown rice penne pasta

Sea salt and freshly ground black pepper

Preheat the oven to 350°F (180°C) and line a baking sheet with foil. Place the pumpkin, onion, and garlic on the baking sheet. Drizzle with olive oil and sprinkle with salt and pepper. Turn the pumpkin cut-side down and pierce a few holes in the skin with a fork. Cover and bake until the onion is soft and the pumpkin flesh is very tender, 35 to 45 minutes. Add the sage to the pan during the last few minutes. Remove the pan from the oven, keeping everything covered, and let it continue to steam for another 10 to 15 minutes.

Pour the vegetable broth into a blender. Remove the skin and add the pumpkin flesh to the blender along with the onion, peeled garlic, sage, cashews, and a few generous pinches of salt and pepper. Blend until creamy. Add the olive oil and blend again. Taste and adjust the seasonings, adding more salt and pepper if you like.

Prepare the pasta according to the instructions on the package, cooking until al dente.

Reserve ½ cup (125 mL) of pasta water before draining the pasta.

Drain the pasta and return it to the pot. Stir in half the sauce, adding more as needed to coat the pasta. Add the reserved pasta water, ¼ cup (60 mL) at a time, to thin the sauce and make it creamy. Taste and season with more salt and pepper. Serve hot.

VEGAN | **GLUTEN-FREE**

SERVES: **4**

Cook once, eat twice! Make butternut squash risotto for two, and save the other half to make these arancini balls the next night.

BUTTERNUT SQUASH RISOTTO & ARANCINI

RISOTTO

1 tablespoon (15 mL) extra-virgin olive oil

1 small yellow onion, chopped

2 cups (500 mL) cubed butternut squash

2 garlic cloves, minced

1 cup (250 mL) uncooked arborio rice

½ cup (125 mL) dry white wine

4 cups (1 L) hot vegetable broth

2 tablespoons (30 mL) butter or olive oil

½ cup (125 mL) freshly grated Parmesan cheese

½ cup (125 mL) fresh herbs (parsley or basil)

Sea salt and freshly ground black pepper

ARANCINI

½ recipe leftover butternut squash risotto (makes about twelve 2-inch [5-cm] balls)

1 cup (250 mL) panko bread crumbs

Simple fresh tomato sauce (page 251) or your favorite marinara sauce, for serving

2 ounces (60 g) smoked mozzarella cheese, cut into twelve small cubes (optional)

In a large skillet, heat the olive oil over medium heat. Add the onion and season with salt and pepper. Cook for 2 to 3 minutes, then add the butternut squash and cook for 6 to 8 minutes. Add the garlic and the rice. Stir and let cook for about 1 minute. Season again with salt and pepper, then add the wine. Stir and cook for 1 to 2 minutes, or until the wine cooks down.

Add the vegetable broth, ¾ cup (175 mL) at a time, stirring continuously, to allow each addition of broth to be absorbed before adding the next. Cook until the butternut squash is tender and the risotto is soft and creamy. Stir in the butter, Parmesan cheese, and fresh herbs. Season to taste and serve immediately. Save leftover risotto in the fridge for arancini.

Preheat the oven to 400°F (200°C) and line a baking sheet with parchment paper.

Remove the risotto from the fridge. Spread the panko on a large plate. Scoop 1 heaping tablespoon (15 mL) of the risotto and use your hands to form a 2-inch (5-cm) ball. Place a piece of smoked mozzarella in the center, if using. Roll each ball in the panko and place on a baking sheet. Bake for 25 minutes or until golden brown and crispy.

Serve with heated simple fresh tomato sauce.

VEGAN: Skip the cheese. | **GLUTEN-FREE:** Use gluten-free panko. | *SERVES:* **4**

26

Zucchini

& SUMMER SQUASH

Zucchini is everyone's favorite vegetable at the beginning of the summer, and then we can't seem to use it up or give it away fast enough. Thankfully, zucchini and summer squash are some of the most versatile vegetables, especially for healthy cooking. The possibilities are endless.

BLEND IT
into zucchini pesto and put it on everything.

SLICE IT
into julienne strips or peel it into thin ribbons to make "noodles."

BAKE IT
into chocolate muffins (your kids will never know).

MAKE
zucchini "ricotta" for a zucchini lasagna.

SEASON

SUMMER

1 Make the zucchini "ricotta" and layer it with tomatoes, zucchini, and lasagna noodles.

2 Layer more zucchini planks and add more tomatoes.

3 Top with cheese, or skip it to make this vegan.

4 Bake and dig in!

ZUCCHINI LASAGNA
WITH ZUCCHINI "RICOTTA"

INGREDIENTS

ZUCCHINI "RICOTTA"

¼ cup (60 mL) chopped walnuts

2 garlic cloves

7 ounces (200 g) extra-firm tofu

½ cup (125 mL) chopped zucchini

1 tablespoon (15 mL) fresh lemon juice

½ teaspoon (2 mL) dried oregano

¼ teaspoon (1 mL) red pepper flakes

½ cup (125 mL) chopped fresh basil

Sea salt and freshly ground black pepper

- -

5 ounces (140 g) brown rice lasagna noodles

Extra-virgin olive oil, for drizzling

1 can (14.5 ounces/411 g) diced tomatoes

2 zucchini, sliced into thin planks

1 cup (250 mL) grated pecorino cheese

Freshly ground black pepper

DIRECTIONS

Preheat the oven to 375°F (190°C).

Make the zucchini "ricotta": In a food processor, combine the walnuts, garlic, tofu, chopped zucchini, lemon juice, oregano, red pepper flakes, basil, and generous pinches of salt and pepper. Process to a spreadable consistency.

Bring a large pot of salted water to a boil. Prepare the pasta according to the instructions on the package, cooking until al dente. Drain and rinse.

Drizzle a 9 x 13-inch (23 x 33-cm) pan with olive oil, then layer the ingredients as follows:

First layer: a third of the tomatoes, half of the noodles, half of the ricotta, half of the zucchini

Second layer: a third of the tomatoes, half of the noodles, half of the ricotta, half of the zucchini

Top with the remaining third of the tomatoes. Sprinkle with the grated cheese and drizzle with olive oil.

Bake, covered, for 15 minutes. Uncover and bake 20 to 30 more minutes, or until the zucchini is tender but still has a bite and the tomatoes and cheese are bubbling. Let rest for 10 minutes before serving. Season with freshly cracked black pepper.

NOTE I promise you'll never taste the tofu in here!

VEGAN: Skip the cheese on top.

GLUTEN-FREE: Use gluten-free lasagna noodles or double zucchini planks.

SERVES: 4

DOUBLE CHOCOLATE
ZUCCHINI MUFFINS

INGREDIENTS

1 tablespoon (15 mL) ground flaxseed

3 tablespoons (45 mL) water

2 teaspoons (10 mL) fresh lemon juice

1 cup (250 mL) almond milk, at room temperature

2 cups (500 mL) spelt flour or a mix of white and wheat

⅓ cup (75 mL) cocoa powder

1 tablespoon (15 mL) baking powder

1 teaspoon (5 mL) baking soda

½ teaspoon (2 mL) sea salt

½ teaspoon (2 mL) cinnamon

¼ teaspoon (1 mL) nutmeg

¼ cup (60 mL) coconut oil, melted

⅔ cup (150 mL) maple syrup

1 teaspoon (5 mL) vanilla extract

½ cup (125 mL) semisweet chocolate chips

1¼ cups (300 mL) finely shredded unpeeled zucchini

DIRECTIONS

Preheat the oven to 350°F (180°C). Line a 12-cup muffin tin with paper liners or spray with nonstick cooking spray.

Combine the ground flaxseed and water and set aside to thicken. Stir the lemon juice into the almond milk and set aside.

In a large bowl, combine the flour, cocoa powder, baking powder, baking soda, salt, cinnamon, and nutmeg. In a medium bowl, whisk together the flaxseed mixture, almond milk/lemon juice mixture, coconut oil, maple syrup, and vanilla.

Pour the wet ingredients into the bowl with the dry ingredients and stir until just combined. Do not overmix. Fold in the chocolate chips and then the zucchini.

Evenly divide the batter into the muffin cups, filling each about three-quarters full, and bake for 14 to 16 minutes, or until a toothpick inserted comes out clean. Cool for 10 minutes, then remove from the pan and place on a wire rack to finish cooling.

VEGAN

YIELD: **12** *MUFFINS*

SUMMER SQUASH & CHERRY TOMATO PASTA

INGREDIENTS

4 medium yellow squash

8 ounces (225 g) capellini or brown rice spaghetti

Extra-virgin olive oil, for drizzling

2 cups (500 mL) cherry tomatoes, halved

1 garlic clove, minced

6 sprigs fresh thyme leaves

Juice of ½ small lemon

Sea salt and freshly ground black pepper

- -

TOPPINGS (CHOOSE 1 OR MORE)

Freshly grated Parmesan cheese

Fresh mozzarella slices

Torn fresh basil leaves

Red pepper flakes

Any pesto from page 275

DIRECTIONS

Use a julienne peeler to slice the squash into long thin strips.

Bring a large pot of salted water to a boil. Prepare the pasta according to the instructions on the package, cooking until al dente. Drain the pasta.

Meanwhile, in a small skillet, heat a drizzle of olive oil over low heat. Add the tomatoes, garlic, fresh thyme, and pinches of salt and pepper. Cook until soft, about 3 minutes, turning as needed.

Toss the pasta with the squash, tomatoes, a drizzle of olive oil, the lemon juice, and a pinch of salt and pepper. Serve with your choice of toppings.

VEGAN | **GLUTEN-FREE**

SERVES: **4**

SUMMER SQUASH SUCCOTASH

1 ear fresh corn, husked

1 tablespoon (15 mL) coconut oil

½ cup (125 mL) chopped red onion

½ cup (125 mL) diced red bell pepper

12 small pattypan squash, sliced in half or quartered (about 1½ cups/375 mL)

6 baby zucchini, chopped into ½-inch (1-cm) pieces (about 1½ cups/375 mL)

½ cup (125 mL) cooked chickpeas, drained and rinsed (page 285)

2 garlic cloves, minced

1 cup (250 mL) cherry tomatoes, sliced in half

1 scallion, diced

½ teaspoon (2 mL) smoked paprika

1 tablespoon (15 mL) fresh lemon juice

Fresh basil

Sea salt and freshly ground black pepper

Slice the kernels off the corn, then use the back of your knife to scrape the juices off of the corncob. Set aside.

Heat the coconut oil in a large skillet over medium heat. Add the onion and a pinch of salt and pepper. Let cook until soft, about 3 minutes, then add the bell pepper and continue to cook for 2 more minutes, stirring occasionally.

Add the squash and zucchini, cut side down (as best you can), and another pinch of salt and pepper and cook for 5 minutes without moving them so they brown on one side. Stir in the chickpeas and cook for 2 more minutes. Stir in the corn, corn juices, and garlic and cook for 1 minute.

Add the cherry tomatoes, scallion, and smoked paprika. Stir and cook 2 to 3 more minutes.

Turn off the heat and stir in the lemon juice and basil. Season to taste.

VEGAN | **GLUTEN-FREE**

SERVES: **4** *AS A SIDE*

PESTO

CHANGE-O

EXTRA-VIRGIN OLIVE OIL
¼ cup (60 mL)

FRESH LEMON JUICE
2 tablespoons (30 mL)

GARLIC
1 clove

+ SEA SALT AND FRESHLY GROUND BLACK PEPPER

THE RECIPE VARIATIONS

1 TRADITIONAL

BASIL
2 cups (500 mL)

+

PINE NUTS
½ cup (125 mL)

+

PARMESAN CHEESE
¼ cup (60 mL)

2 PEPITA

CILANTRO
2 cups (500 mL)

+

PEPITAS
½ cup (125 mL)

+

GROUND CUMIN +
DRIZZLE OF HONEY
½ teaspoon (2 mL)

3 ZUCCHINI

BASIL
1 cup (250 mL)

+

WALNUTS
½ cup (125 mL)

+

CHOPPED ZUCCHINI
1 cup (250 mL)

4 MINT

MINT
1 cup (250 mL)

+

PISTACHIOS
½ cup (125 mL)

+

PEAS
1 cup (250 mL)

HOMEMADE
HUMMUS

SHARED INGREDIENTS

COOKED CHICKPEAS
1½ cups (375 mL)

EXTRA-VIRGIN OLIVE OIL
2 tablespoons (30 mL)

\+

FRESH LEMON JUICE
2 tablespoons (30 mL)

\+

GARLIC
1 clove

TAHINI
2 tablespoons (30 mL)

\+

WARM WATER
2 to 3 tablespoons (30 to 45 mL)

\+

**SEA SALT AND
FRESHLY GROUND
BLACK PEPPER**

276

1 — PEA & AVOCADO

AVOCADO
1 small

PEAS
½ cup (125 mL)

CUMIN
¼ teaspoon (1 mL)

2 — SWEET POTATO

SWEET POTATO
½ small cooked

MAPLE SYRUP
2 teaspoons (10 mL)

CHILI POWDER
1 to 2 teaspoons (4 to 8 mL)

3 — RED PEPPER

1 ROASTED RED PEPPER
¼ to ⅓ cup (60 to 75 mL)

TOASTED ALMONDS
¼ cup (60 mL)

SMOKED PAPRIKA
½ teaspoon (2 mL)

4 — ARTICHOKE

ARTICHOKE HEARTS
1 cup (250 mL)

BASIL
¼ cup (60 mL)

MINT
¼ cup (60 mL)

HOLY GUACAMOLE

3 AVOCADOS   +   JUICE OF 1 LIME

+ GENEROUS PINCHES OF COARSE SEA SALT

THE RECIPE VARIATIONS

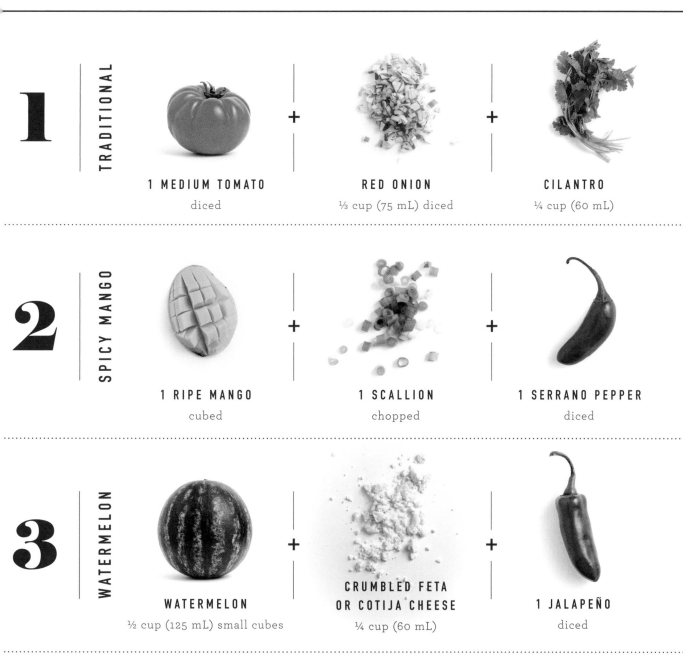

1 — TRADITIONAL

1 MEDIUM TOMATO
diced

+

RED ONION
⅓ cup (75 mL) diced

+

CILANTRO
¼ cup (60 mL)

2 — SPICY MANGO

1 RIPE MANGO
cubed

+

1 SCALLION
chopped

+

1 SERRANO PEPPER
diced

3 — WATERMELON

WATERMELON
½ cup (125 mL) small cubes

+

**CRUMBLED FETA
OR COTIJA CHEESE**
¼ cup (60 mL)

+

1 JALAPEÑO
diced

4 — CHIPOTLE APPLE

1 CHIPOTLE
(from a can) diced

+

1 GALA APPLE
diced

+

CILANTRO
¼ cup (60 mL)

Salsa

SHARED INGREDIENTS

JUICE OF 1 TO 2 LIMES
at least
1 tablespoon (15 mL),
more to taste,
plus a little zest

CILANTRO
¼ to ⅓ cup
(60 to 75 mL)
chopped

RED ONION
¼ cup (60 mL)
chopped

GARLIC
½ to 1 clove

**PINCH OF SUGAR OR
¼ TEASPOON (1 ML) HONEY**
(skip with the fruit salsas)

+

**GENEROUS PINCHES OF SEA SALT AND
FRESHLY GROUND BLACK PEPPER**
at least ½ teaspoon (2 mL)

1   SALSA FRESCA

 +  +

3 MEDIUM TOMATOES
diced

¼ TO ½ JALAPEÑO
diced

1 SCALLION
chopped

2   CREAMY TOMATILLO

 +  +

4 ROASTED TOMATILLOS

AVOCADO
1 small

¼ TO ½ SERRANO

3   MANGO-BASIL

 +  +

1 RIPE MANGO
cubed

BASIL
4 leaves sliced

SRIRACHA
1 teaspoon (5 mL)

4   SPICY PEACH

 +  +

4 RIPE PEACHES
diced

GINGER
½ teaspoon (2 mL)

2 THAI CHILES
diced

SMOOTHIES

1 BANANA
frozen

ALMOND MILK
1 cup (250 mL),
more as needed

+ HANDFUL OF ICE

THE RECIPE VARIATIONS

1   BERRY MINT

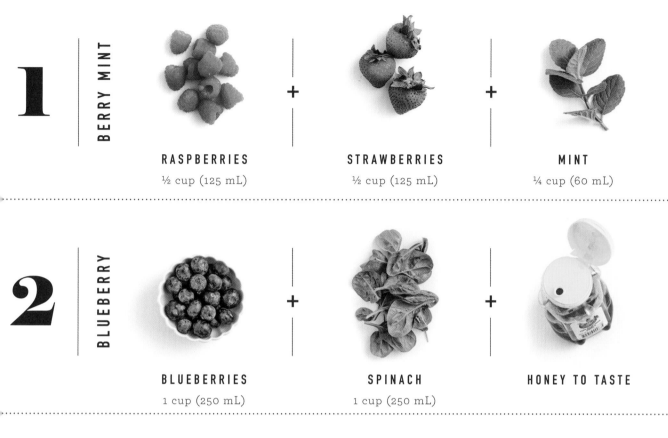

RASPBERRIES
½ cup (125 mL)

+

STRAWBERRIES
½ cup (125 mL)

+

MINT
¼ cup (60 mL)

2   BLUEBERRY

BLUEBERRIES
1 cup (250 mL)

+

SPINACH
1 cup (250 mL)

+

HONEY TO TASTE

3   GINGER PEACH

2 RIPE PEACHES

+

GRATED GINGER
½ teaspoon (2 mL)

+

JUICE OF 1 LIME

4   CHERRY CACAO

TART CHERRIES
1 cup (250 mL)

+

CACAO POWDER
2 tablespoons (30 mL)

+

MAPLE SYRUP
1 tablespoon (15 mL)

GRAINS

Start by rinsing your grains. Place your dry grains in a strainer that fits inside of a bowl and rinse a few times until the water in the bowl is clear. Drain and you're ready to cook.

When I cook grains, I like to make a big batch and store extra in the fridge for handy quick-cooking meals throughout the week. You can use most grains interchangeably—for instance, a recipe that uses farro will also work with wheat berries or brown rice. If you're gluten-free, use quinoa or millet in place of other grains.

A note about rice: I prefer to use a rice cooker. Even with an inexpensive rice cooker, you can walk away and forget about it and have perfectly cooked rice.

FARRO

1 cup (250 mL) dry + pot full of water = 3 cups (750 mL) cooked

Bring a pot of water to a boil. Add the rinsed farro. Reduce the heat and simmer for 30 to 40 minutes, or until tender. Drain.

HARD WHEAT BERRIES

1 cup (250 mL) dry + pot full of water = about 3 cups (750 mL) cooked

Bring a pot of water to a boil. Add the rinsed wheat berries. Reduce the heat and simmer for 45 to 90 minutes, or until tender. Drain.

MILLET

1 cup (250 mL) dry + 2 cups (500 mL) water = 3½ cups (875 mL) cooked

Add the rinsed millet to a dry pot. Over medium heat, toast for 1 to 2 minutes. Stir, add water, and bring to a boil. Cover, reduce heat, and simmer for 15 minutes. Remove from the heat and let it sit, covered, for 10 more minutes. Fluff with a fork.

QUINOA

1 cup (250 mL) dry + 1¾ cups (425 mL) water = 3 cups (750 mL) cooked

Add the rinsed quinoa and water to a medium pot. Bring to a boil, cover, reduce the heat, and simmer for 15 minutes. Remove from the heat and let it sit, covered, for 10 more minutes. Fluff with a fork.

SHORT-GRAIN BROWN RICE

1 cup (250 mL) dry + 2 cups (500 mL) water + 1 teaspoon (5 mL) extra-virgin olive oil = 3 cups (750 mL) cooked

Combine the rinsed rice, water, and olive oil in a pot and bring to a boil. Cover, reduce the heat, and simmer for 45 minutes. Remove from the heat and let it sit, covered, for 10 more minutes. Fluff with a fork.

SOFT WHEAT BERRIES

1 cup (250 mL) dry + 3 cups (750 mL) water = about 3 cups (750 mL) cooked

Bring the water to a boil. Add the rinsed wheat berries. Cover, reduce the heat, and simmer for 25 to 30 minutes, or until tender. Drain any excess water.

WHITE JASMINE OR BASMATI RICE

1 cup (250 mL) dry + 1½ cups (375 mL) water + 1 teaspoon (5 mL) extra-virgin olive oil = 3 cups (750 mL) cooked

Combine the rinsed rice, water, and olive oil in a pot and bring to a boil. Cover, reduce the heat, and simmer for 15 minutes. Remove from the heat and let it sit, covered, for 10 more minutes. Fluff with a fork.

BEANS

1 cup (250 mL) dry = 2½ to 3 cups (750 mL) cooked

Place the beans in a large bowl and pick out and discard any stones or debris. Cover the beans with 2 to 3 inches (5 to 7.5 cm) of water and discard any beans that float. Soak at room temperature for 8 hours or overnight. Drain and rinse the beans well and place in a large pot. Cover the beans with 2 to 3 inches (5 to 7.5 cm) of cold water. Place the pot over high heat and bring to a boil. Lower the heat and simmer, covered, until the beans have softened. This can take anywhere from 1 to 2 hours. The age of your beans, the variety, and the size can all affect the cooking time. Begin checking for doneness after 1 hour. The beans are cooked when they are soft enough to mash easily with a fork. Drain and cool.

TOASTING NUTS

In a small skillet over low heat, add the nuts and a pinch of sea salt. Toast, stirring occasionally, until the nuts are golden brown. Depending on the intensity of the heat on your stove, allow about 2 minutes for larger ones (almonds, walnuts, cashews), 1 minute for smaller ones (pistachios, peanuts), and about 30 seconds for pine nuts.

Hazelnuts: Preheat the oven to 275°F (135°C). Place the nuts on a baking sheet and roast for 20 to 30 minutes, or until the skins crack open and their texture softens. Shortcut this step by buying pre-roasted unsalted hazelnuts or blanched hazelnuts.

HOMEMADE PIZZA DOUGH

¾ cup (175 mL) warm (105 to 115°F/40 to 46°C) water

1 teaspoon (5 mL) honey or cane sugar

1 packet (¼ ounce/7 g) active dry yeast

1 cup (250 mL) spelt or whole wheat flour, plus more as needed

1 cup (250 mL) all-purpose flour

1 teaspoon (5 mL) sea salt

2 tablespoons (30 mL) extra-virgin olive oil

¼ cup (60 mL) cornmeal

In a small bowl, stir together ¼ cup (60 mL) of the water and the honey, then sprinkle in the yeast. Let stand until foamy, about 5 minutes. If it doesn't foam, start over with new yeast.

In the bowl of a stand mixer with a dough hook attached, combine the spelt flour, all-purpose flour, and salt. Add the yeast mixture, the remaining ½ cup (125 mL) of water, and 1 tablespoon (15 mL) of the oil. Mix on medium speed until the dough forms into a ball around the hook. If the dough is too sticky, add a little more flour. Turn the dough out onto a lightly floured surface and gently knead into a smooth ball.

Brush the inside of a large bowl with the remaining 1 tablespoon (15 mL) of olive oil. Place the dough in the bowl and cover with plastic wrap. Set the bowl in a warm spot until the dough has doubled in size, about 1 hour.

Turn the dough out onto a floured surface. Punch it down and form it into a ball. Cover it with a kitchen towel and let it rest for 10 more minutes.

Stretch and bake according to the pizza recipe you are using (roasted cauliflower and pear pizza, page 105, or spring onion pizzas, page 181).

If not using immediately, seal with plastic wrap and refrigerate overnight or up to 2 days. Let stand at room temperature for 1 hour before using.

Yield: Makes 1 pound (450 g) dough, enough for one large or two small pizzas.

VEGAN: Use maple syrup instead of honey.

SAUCES, SPREADS, DRESSINGS, ETC.

CASHEW CREAM

1 cup (250 mL) raw unsalted cashews, soaked 3 to 4 hours, preferably overnight, drained and rinsed

½ cup (125 mL) water

1 garlic clove

2 tablespoons (30 mL) fresh lemon juice

2 tablespoons (30 mL) extra-virgin olive oil

½ teaspoon (2 mL) sea salt

Blend until smooth.

SUN "CHEESE"

1¼ cups (300 mL) hulled sunflower seeds, soaked 3 to 4 hours, preferably overnight, drained and rinsed

1 cup (250 mL) water

1 garlic clove

2 tablespoons (30 mL) white wine vinegar

1 tablespoon (15 mL) fresh lemon juice, plus a bit of zest

½ teaspoon (2 mL) sea salt

Blend until smooth.

Variation: Add 1 to 2 peppers from canned chipotles in adobo sauce to make chipotle sun "cheese."

PEANUT SAUCE

3 tablespoons (45 mL) natural peanut butter (creamy or crunchy)

1 tablespoon (15 mL) toasted sesame oil

1½ teaspoons (7 mL) tamari

1 teaspoon (5 mL) freshly grated ginger

1 garlic clove, minced

1 teaspoon (5 mL) sriracha

2 tablespoons (30 mL) water

In a small bowl, stir to combine.

Variations: Substitute with almond butter or cashew butter.

MANY-HERB SAUCE

7 ounces (200 g) Greek yogurt

⅔ cup (150 mL) chopped leafy herbs and stems (e.g., cilantro, basil, tarragon)

2 scallions, chopped

½ garlic clove

Juice of 1 lime

1 tablespoon (15 mL) extra-virgin olive oil

Sea salt and freshly ground black pepper

½ teaspoon (2 mL) honey (optional)

Pulse in a food processor.

Vegan option: Use maple syrup instead of honey and cashew cream or sun "cheese" in place of yogurt.

CHILI-SPICED YOGURT

½ cup (125 mL) Greek yogurt
1 to 2 teaspoons (5 to 10 mL) chili powder
2 teaspoons (10 mL) fresh lime juice
¼ teaspoon (1 mL) honey
Sea salt and freshly ground black pepper

In a small bowl, stir to combine.

Vegan option: Substitute maple syrup for honey and cashew cream or sun "cheese" (page 286) in place of yogurt.

LEMON-DIJON DRESSING

2 tablespoons (30 mL) extra-virgin olive oil
2 tablespoons (30 mL) fresh lemon juice
2 tablespoons (30 mL) fresh orange juice
1 teaspoon (5 mL) Dijon mustard
1 garlic clove, minced
Sea salt and freshly ground black pepper

In a small bowl, stir to combine.

SWEET CHILI SAUCE

1 tablespoon (15 mL) tamari
2 tablespoons (30 mL) water
1 tablespoon (15 mL) cane sugar
2 small garlic cloves, minced
2 teaspoons (10 mL) fresh lime juice
2 teaspoons (10 mL) rice vinegar
½ teaspoon (2 mL) red pepper flakes

In a small bowl, stir to combine.

CARROT-GINGER SAUCE

1 cup (250 mL) chopped raw carrots
1 garlic clove
¼ cup (60 mL) extra-virgin olive oil
2 tablespoons (30 mL) tahini
2 tablespoons (30 mL) fresh lemon juice
1 teaspoon (5 mL) minced ginger
2 tablespoons (30 mL) fresh orange juice
Sea salt and freshly ground black pepper

In a blender, puree the carrots with the garlic, olive oil, tahini, lemon juice, ginger, and orange juice. Season with salt and pepper.

COCONUT CREAM

2 (14-ounce/414-mL) cans full-fat coconut milk, refrigerated overnight
⅓ cup (75 mL) sifted powdered sugar
Few drops of vanilla extract

Remove the coconut milk from the fridge and carefully scoop the thick solid part off the top. Save the watery part for another use. Use an electric mixer to whip the coconut cream until fluffy, 3 to 5 minutes. Add the powdered sugar and vanilla and mix again.

Variations: Add ½ teaspoon (2 mL) cinnamon, ½ teaspoon (2 mL) lemon zest, or a few drops of lemon oil.

THANK YOU.

To my small and mighty team of the most talented, hardworking people I know:

To my husband, Jack, for going with the flow that day in 2011 when I handed you a camera and its manual and said, "We're starting a food blog." For patiently putting up with late-night shoots, cold food, and my occasional meltdown when that napkin just wouldn't go in the right place.

To my mom, my number one fan, thank you for supporting every one of my creative ambitions. Thank you for being our very first blog reader and for tirelessly proofreading every last word of this book. Thank you for flying in when things got crazy. For washing truckloads of dishes, running countless errands, feeding the dogs when we'd forget, and for picking out the perfect cauliflower for page 96.

To Trina Bentley, for designing the most beautiful book possible. As always, I love our seamless collaboration where words aren't usually even necessary.

To Jenn Elliott Blake, for packing up (literally so many boxes) and flying to Austin when I needed your help most. I'm in awe of your talent and eye for the tiniest prop styling details. These pages are infinitely more beautiful because of you.

To Judy Linden, my amazing book agent, for encouraging me to create a book in the first place. Thank you for guiding me through this crazy process.

To Lucia Watson, my wonderful editor, thank you for your passion, support, and encouragement. Also, thank you to Andrea Magyar and the entire Penguin dream team. I'm still pinching myself for this opportunity to work together.

Thank you to the vegetable farmers in Austin whose produce adorns these pages— everyone at the SFC farmers market, Rain Lily Farm, The Farmhouse Delivery, Tecolote Farm, and Johnson's Backyard Garden.

Most important, thank you to the *Love & Lemons* blog readers! This book is for you and also because of you.

— EASY, SEASONAL —
VEGETARIAN RECIPES *that make*
INSPIRED EVERYDAY COOKING
— ATTAINABLE —

LOVE & LEMONS

— EVERY DAY —

On Sale April 2019